THE HEART OF LOVE

How to Go Beyond Fantasy to Find True Relationship Fulfillment

Dr. John F. Demartini

HAY HOUSE, INC.
Carlsbad, California
London • Sydney • Johannesburg
Vancouver • Hong Kong • New Delhi

Published and distributed in the United States by: Hay House, Inc.: www.hayhouse.com • **Published and distributed in Australia by:** Hay House Australia Pty. Ltd.: www.hayhouse.com.au • **Published and distributed in the United Kingdom by:** Hay House UK, Ltd.: www.hayhouse.co.uk • **Published and distributed in the Republic of South Africa by:** Hay House SA (Pty), Ltd.: orders@psdprom.co.za • **Distributed in Canada by:** Raincoast: www.raincoast.com • **Published in India by:** Hay House Publications (India) Pvt. Ltd.: www.hayhouseindia.co.in

Design: Nick C. Welch

The Demartini Method and *The Breakthrough Experience* are registered trademarks of Dr. John F. Demartini.

The people in the stories in this book are, in some cases, composites. In every case, names have been changed to protect the privacy of the individuals.

The author of this book does not dispense medical advice or prescribe the use of any technique as a form of treatment for physical, emotional, or medical problems without the advice of a physician, either directly or indirectly. The intent of the author is only to offer information of a general nature to help you in your quest for emotional and spiritual well-being. In the event you use any of the information in this book for yourself, which is your constitutional right, the author and the publisher assume no responsibility for your actions.

Library of Congress Cataloging-in-Publication Data

Demartini, John F.
  The heart of love : how to go beyond fantasy to find true relationship fulfillment / John F. Demartini.
    p. cm.
  ISBN-13: 978-1-4019-1232-1 (tradepaper)
1. Man-woman relationships. 2. Love. 3. Mate selection. I. Title.
HQ801.D46 2007
  306.73'4--dc22

                      2006024681

ISBN: 978-1-4019-1232-1

10 09 08 07   4 3 2 1
1st edition, January 2007

Printed in the United States of America

The
Heart of
Love

Other Hay House Titles by Dr. John F. Demartini

The Breakthrough Experience:
A Revolutionary New Approach to Personal Transformation

Count Your Blessings:
The Healing Power of Gratitude and Love

How to Make One Hell of a Profit and Still Get to Heaven

You Can Have an Amazing Life . . . in Just 60 Days!

All of the above are available at your local bookstore,
or may be ordered by visiting:

Hay House USA: **www.hayhouse.com**®
Hay House Australia: **www.hayhouse.com.au**
Hay House UK: **www.hayhouse.co.uk**
Hay House South Africa: **orders@psdprom.co.za**
Hay House India: **www.hayhouseindia.co.in**

CONTENTS

INTRODUCTION

*All paths lead to the same goal: to convey
to others what we are.*
— Pablo Neruda

When I first met Joe, he was attending one of my seminars in a large midwestern city in the United States. After the program ended, he told me that he'd had such a realization and transformation that he wanted to send his wife, Adele, to me for a private consultation.

At the time, I was living in New York City, so Adele flew to the Big Apple, and we met in her hotel suite. I like to joke that we spent one magical day in a hotel room together, and when you hear the rest of the story, you'll understand why Joe always chuckles with genuine appreciation.

Why had her husband thought it would be important for us to talk? Adele told me, "We're not getting along, we have a lot of fights, and our relationship is on the edge."

I asked her a series of questions and took her through a number of processes, all of which you're going to read about in this book. I also helped her see how she could communicate more effectively with Joe, in terms of his values instead of just her own. I showed her how to see the world through his eyes and taught her ways that she could help him be receptive to doing the same for her.

Adele told me that she believed Joe's highest values— what was most important to him—were work, money, cars, golf, and certain friends. She also revealed what meant the most to her (which certainly were special, but aren't as crucial to this story). We spent the lion's share of the day *linking* her values and his so that she could see that whatever he does actually helps her do what she loves, and vice versa. Near the end of our time together, we rehearsed dialogues where she communicated in the new way she'd just learned, practicing conveying her values in terms of his so that he'd feel more important and understood, without sacrificing what was truly significant to her.

After she left New York, Adele stopped at a sporting-goods store on her way back from the airport. As soon as she walked through the door of her home, she dropped her bags, ran to Joe, and threw her arms around him, telling him that she loved him and that she'd picked up some golf balls, a golf shirt, and his favorite golf magazine for him.

She smiled at his surprise and announced: "I noticed you had the big tournament coming up. And you know how every year you want to go, and every year I bitch at you because it's always a weekend I wanted to spend with you and the kids?

"Well, I realized that there's a big sale happening in London that same weekend this year. My mother's been talking with me about it, and I thought maybe the kids and I could all go there together. They could see their grandparents, we could save money on their school clothes, and I could bring back some really novel items for the house, too, that no one else has around here. You'd have a blast at the tournament, and I'd have fun with the family and shopping—so there'd be no bitching. I want you to have a good time golfing with your friends, honey."

As she kept talking with him about how they'd make new connections overseas that would help him in his profession, how she'd save money, how they could enjoy test-driving some of those European cars he was curious about, and how he'd play golf with his friends, all Joe could say was, "Wow, sure. That sounds great!" In the end, he gave her the credit card to book the flights, and then he sent me a thank-you note.

He wrote to me how "different" Adele was, how close they'd become, and how they'd reignited their intimacy. He expressed his gratitude for "whatever you did with my wife."

That magical day in her hotel room, all I did was teach Adele how to speak in Joe's language of love and show her how that would help her materialize what she wanted to have in her life, too.

This wasn't a unique situation. As I travel the world and speak with thousands of people each year, I see certain tendencies, particularly in the area of relationships. Whether I'm conducting a small-scale seminar in Boston; addressing a huge crowd in Toronto; or chatting with people on a talk show in Johannesburg, South Africa, certain patterns emerge. Although cultural differences exist (such as the acceptance or rejection of such practices as polygamy), commonalities are more abundant; and they cross-pollinate all types of relationships: with family members, with co-workers, with romantic partners, with oneself, and even with the universe.

In particular, I've observed that most people live in a fantasy about what they're going to get out of their bonds with others. Frequently, this comes from several mistaken ideas about why and how they "should" be with someone. Usually, they think the purpose of relationships is to make them happy, and the way to do it is to get others to adopt their value systems and act accordingly.

In other words, people regularly and quite unconsciously project their beliefs onto others, expecting friends, lovers, children, and colleagues to live according to a set of ethics and morals that reflect their own values instead of the other person's. They set themselves up to experience perceived disappointment and even betrayal in this way, because we can live only by our own inner compass, not anybody else's. And then they think that other people, or even the universe, do things "to" them, instead of acknowledging that they've created this illusion by not recognizing and honoring what's important to someone else.

There are two things that other people can't and won't live up to: your values and your fantasies. Realize that no truth is ever revealed nor love ever unveiled until cause equals effect synchronously in space-time, meaning that you're your own cause of your own effect at any one moment. In other words, at exactly the instant you perceive an effect (the feeling of being betrayed), *you* are its cause due to your projecting unrealistic expectations onto others that don't match their immediate needs and values. They have the right to alter their decisions, according to their values and in relationship to their changing environment—and at times they will. They'll only live according to their values, *not yours*.

Don't fall into the illusion that anyone else is obligated to live according to what's important to you in any way or at any time, even when they say that they intend to. If they do, be grateful. But if they don't, be unsurprised; they're just being true to themselves and making decisions accordingly.

This book will redefine what loyalty and commitment really mean, helping you understand how to align your values rather than foist them onto others. It will debunk the myths of relationships, aid you in letting go of your fantasies so that you can begin focusing on fulfillment instead, and give step-by-step instructions for linking values systems with other people. We'll also explore sexual dynamics (including the "mysteries" of monogamy and long-term satisfaction) and how they're driven by values; as well as discover new perspectives on dealing with the grief of death, divorce, and other potentially painful relationship "endings."

In 2002, I addressed the subject of relationships in a chapter of my book *The Breakthrough Experience,*[1] but people who attend my seminars, including the one specifically about relationships, have consistently told me that they'd love to have more. Why are relationships so confusing? How can you make sense of them? Most important, how can you become aware of the magnificence that resides in the seeming chaos of your life?

Our connections with one another, although incredibly rich with potential, seem to be one of the most misunderstood areas of life. Many of the people I meet are mired in their ideas about what makes a "good" or "successful" relationship. To paraphrase Ralph Waldo Emerson, the mind becomes hemmed into a thought until a greater thought comes along . . . all governed by the soul. The greater thought I'm offering you is that you can stop kidding yourself about what relationships are and can become, as well as who you are and what others "should" or "must" be in order to experience fulfillment. You can wake up to the fact that not only do you participate in creating your reality, but you also take part in forging your relationships. Neither "just happen" to you, for you're the author of your existence.

---

[1]That book complements this one, and you may find that you'd like to read it, too, especially if you'd love to understand more about how you participate with your reality. If you've already read it, you'll find similar themes here, but in specific ways to apply what you've learned in your relationships.

This book will help you understand what really drives human behavior in romance, business, and families; and it will assure you that you can have the kind of relationships you'll love, whether they're lasting or brief, intensely intimate, or just for fun. In the following pages, I'll share the science of successful and fulfilling communication—the cornerstone of any good relationship—and give you the tools you need to create powerful partnerships with people who can help you acknowledge, experience, and express more of your true self.

Before you dive into the first chapter, let me caution you that this book isn't about self-improvement, which is an illusion anyway. As you'll soon discover, there's nothing about you that needs to be fixed; and every time you grow, there's an element of withering, too—that's as it's designed to be. So please set aside any ideas about getting "better" or "improving." Forget gaining or losing the traits you think will make you the perfect lover, parent, or friend. Simply commit to finding your way to the heart of love.

Open your mind and soul with me, and I can promise that we'll get there together.

✹✹✹ ✹✹✹

CHAPTER ONE

Once Upon a Time, There Were Ten Relationship Myths

*As he drew near the place, he heard a voice that sounded
familiar. He went towards it; Rapunzel saw him, knew him,
and running to him, threw her arms around his neck and wept.
Two of her tears fell on his eyes, and his sight immediately became
clear, and he saw as well as ever. He led her away to
his kingdom, where they were received with great rejoicing,
and lived long in happiness and content.*
— From Ella Boldey's translation of "Rapunzel, or the Maid with
the Golden Hair," a story in *Grimm's Household Fairy Tales*

Every soul sings the song of love. You were created for
this feeling, which neither begins nor ends but simply
is. Love shows no partiality and is its own reward. It can't
be possessed, nor does it possess. It withholds nothing, and
with it, there's no limit. Anything other than this is illusion.
To understand true love is to embrace all.

In some fairy tales, though, this delight becomes a
beast. From the time we're children, these stories and other
misleading fantasies teach us what true love is "supposed"
to be. Who hasn't heard about "happily ever after"? Who
doesn't think it's immature and simplistic? But who hasn't
come under its spell and believed, even just a little, that the
familiar phrase signifies some truth about how caring for
someone "ought" to be?

If you're like most people, you probably buy into at least one of the common cultural myths—our modern-day fairy tales—that can mislead you in your most important relationships. If you continue to believe in any of these untruths, they'll interfere with your life like some nasty old witch with a magic mirror and a poisoned apple. They'll shape your expectations and make you feel as if everyone else gets the fairy tale but you. You'll be living in a monstrous falsehood, "suffering" from it, and feeling and acting as if all of this were true when it doesn't have to be that way for you.

President John F. Kennedy once pointed out, "The great enemy of the truth is very often not the lie—deliberate, contrived, and dishonest—but the myth—persistent, persuasive, and unrealistic." He went on to say that the way out of the woods is to stop enjoying "the comfort of opinion without the discomfort of thought." Are you willing to shine light into the dark corners of your mind and confront myths head-on? If so, you'll get to step out of unfulfilling fantasy and into something far more inspiring: true life, true relationships . . . and true love.

Perhaps you don't think that you're caught up in any false ideas. Please take a moment to consider whether you agree with any of the following statements:

1. A (new) relationship will make me happy.

2. When I find my soul mate, I'll feel complete.

3. The right relationship will last forever.

4. Once we get past these rough waters, it will be smooth sailing.

5. A good relationship requires sacrifice.

6. Great sex happens only at the beginning of a relationship.

7. In the right relationship, I won't have to work at it.

8. If I'm not involved with someone, I'll be lonely.

9. Children complete a marriage.

10. Opposites attract.

Believe it or not, every one of these statements contains a fantasy, a falsehood. In this book, I'll help you see how buying into these childish ideas stunts your personal growth and keeps you from fully experiencing the riches every relationship has to offer. Let's start by taking each of them apart and finding out the truth.

Myth #1: A (New) Relationship Will Make Me Happy

If you've ever been in business or in love with someone beyond that initial period of infatuation, you already know that relationships don't make you happy. Instead, sometimes you perceive yourself to be feeling better, and sometimes you don't—the same as when you're on your own.

Have you ever thought that something would make you happy (a new job or house, for example), and then when you experienced it, you discovered another set of crazies, a fresh set of challenges? You finally received something you wanted, and then you found all-new aggravations and problems. What's more, your fantasy may have set you up for a fall, such as when you romanticize an event to such a degree that the actual day-to-day activities following it can't possibly measure up. No matter what this "thing" was that you thought you'd love to experience, you probably had other moments that you perceived as being pleasant, too . . . and moments of sadness, followed by gladness again.

I'm fond of saying that the "prepartum reds" become those postpartum blues, that the fantasy of parenting contributes to the depression that sets in when you realize that a baby isn't only a bundle of joy but also brings its share of sorrow. Of course, this phenomenon presents itself in more areas than just childbirth. How many newlyweds have been so wrapped up in the wedding plans that the actual marriage seems like a letdown? How many people finish their schooling, get the promotion, buy that car, or what have you and are surprised that it doesn't permanently assure their happiness?

Regardless of the circumstances, everyone oscillates between feeling up and down throughout their entire lives, and you'll experience both sensations in every relationship, no matter how ideally it begins. You'll have periods of comfort and discomfort. At times, you'll be treated with what you perceive to be kindness, and you'll also receive what at the time appears to be cruelty, no matter how "wonderful" or "beautiful" your mate may seem to be.

Happiness isn't the reason for being with someone, anyway. **The purpose of relationships is to help awaken you to the inherent balance existing within and around you, and to assist you in acknowledging your own magnificence and wholeness.** In fact, after the initial crush wears off, your disillusionment (the realization that *Oh, boy—this one isn't going to make me happy either*) serves as a reminder of this basic truth.

During the infatuation phase, you see mostly one side of the coin—the attraction, positive traits, and potential for happily ever after—but that's delusional. This phenomenon of selective perception of positives is so common that psychologists have a name for it: the "pink-lens effect." Ever hear of rose-colored glasses? Likewise, as a relationship matures, you can choose to see the negatives for the most part, but that's equally delusional. (A blue lens, perhaps?)

Both of these phases reflect imbalanced perspectives, and neither can be called true love. To experience the heart of love, you're wise to moderate the two extremes of infatuation (which breeds fear of loss and desperation) and resentment (which breeds distrust and disparagement). You learn to neither cling to someone else nor long for something that you perceive you don't have; you feel grateful for what and who are in your life right now. You love what *is*.

This doesn't erase the ups and downs, the ticktock of emotions. Instead, it dampens or narrows the oscillation. In your life, and because of yourself and no one else, you'll still be happy and sad, accepting and rejecting, nice and mean, generous and greedy, polite and rude, and so on. You'll be and feel *all of this,* because that's just how humans are: We require both complementary sides of life to thrive.

Actual experience is far more inspiring than illusion and fantasy. How wonderful that you don't just order up your emotional life and have it delivered to you like some relationship pizza. How magnificent that you, all by yourself, get to explore the incredible array of passions unique to humanity—and that connecting with others helps you expand into an ever-increasing capacity to feel, think, and experience. How amazing it is that other people don't give you your experience of life, but can help you become more deeply aware of it!

When you approach relationships with all this in mind, your appreciation will be radically increased. Instead of getting disappointed because you're not happy all the time, you can start to identify all the facets of your life and grow from that experience, whether you'll be sharing your days with someone else or not; and if so, whether it's for a long time or just a little while.

Myth #2: When I Find My Soul Mate, I'll Feel Complete

As you'll explore in much more detail later in this book, there's no such thing as one forever, fantasy-fulfilling person who'll give you everything that you think you need. Rather than encourage you to look for a certain someone to fill whatever voids you perceive in your life, I'll help you learn to find resources inside yourself and to see them in many people around you.

Carrying on as if your one and only soul mate will complete you leads to so-called heartbreak, although it's not really your heart that gets broken. Rather, it's the false ideas that you project onto your "loved" ones. You experience a "broken heart" only when you've been infatuated and now perceive loss of some kind. And when the fantasy falls apart, you'll tend to resent someone else for not making it come true. Yet you set yourself up for that disappointment right from the start by denying the negatives, exaggerating the positives, and placing the other person on a pedestal. When that special someone behaves as any other normal human being would—by displaying both apparently positive and negative traits—he or she gets yanked down off the pedestal and thrown into the pit.

This is when people say things such as:

"I thought he was *the one*, but then he . . ."

"I thought she was *different from all the others,*
but then she . . ."
You can fill in the rest.

Thinking that someone will know and love you so well that any negative traits will disappear sets you up for a fall. That doesn't mean there's no such thing as a soul mate, just that we're wise to redefine the term.

A soul mate is actually your full complement. This may be unified and expressed at any moment in one individual or be diversified into many people. This being participates in your expressing your wholeness. Here's another way to put it: **The soul mate helps you awaken to and love all components of yourself.** This assists you in discovering and appreciating any of your disowned parts. But don't fall down the rabbit hole and start thinking that someone else "fills in" your "missing" parts. There's nothing lacking in you!

Your soul mate can be someone (or "some many") with whom you merge and from whom you emerge as an individual. When you truly find this, you discern that the other person is (or other people are) no more the source of fulfillment than one star is the source of light for another. Yet two or more stars together shine beautifully full of light.

We'll be exploring the topic of soul mates in more depth later on, and I promise you some mind-blowing perspectives. For now, let me leave you with this: Your soul mate is around you 24 hours a day. At the end of this book, you'll understand completely that instead of endlessly searching, you can discover that being (or those beings). You'll also discover how you're constantly manifesting your soul mate according to the values you hold throughout your life.

Myth #3: The Right Relationship Will Last Forever

What if I told you that for every relationship coming together, there's one falling apart? This is certainly supported by the often-quoted statistic that half of all marriages end in divorce. And in countries where religious reasons prevent formal dissolution, there are affairs and forms of polygamy, which are really divorce processes without legal papers.

Having this fantasy that you're supposed to stay together forever can be disheartening when you know there's only a 50-50 probability of doing so. (Of course, when you add in the fact that in most relationships one partner dies before the other, the likelihood of spending your entire life with someone approaches zero percent.)

The right relationship lasts as long as both people in it would love it to last. If you'd love the kind of bond that stretches "as long as we both shall live," you'll be gaining some skills and methods for achieving that in this book. But keep in mind that there are no guarantees, and no matter what you do, it will most certainly not bring you a life of pure perceived happiness. No, you'll grow old together for better and worse, in sickness and health, and feeling richer and poorer. You'll experience the full array of complementary opposites.

The key is not letting your commitment to weathering any storms cloud your perceptions about what's currently happening. Two predictable problems stem directly from buying into the myth of forever:

1. Taking someone for granted because you think this person has to stay with you no matter what

2. Feeling devastated and depressed if a breakup occurs and the fantasy self-destructs ("But I thought we'd always be together")

The idea that a relationship "ending" is the equivalent of failing is a childish notion. If you can embrace the idea that the purpose of being with someone is to bring you to a greater understanding and appreciation of yourself, you begin to realize that "forever" is a ridiculous standard—unless you're talking about the human heart and soul, which do remain connected no matter what. It's the understatement of this century to say that things in physical form change, but it's nowhere more evident than in relationships. Death, estrangement, divorce, and even amicable distancing—these are all common so-called endings to a relationship.

It's worth pointing out, though, that these apparent endings are mere illusions to the human heart and soul. Quantum physics shows that two particles once connected remain so, as entangled partners, even when they're removed from one another. John Stewart Bell, an Irish physicist, identified this phenomenon in the 1960s and called it *nonlocality.* In other words, the connection has to do with something that's "not here." So from a scientific perspective, there's no such thing as an end to a relationship of the human heart, which is a form of energy (which is particles and waves). This could be likened to what Albert Einstein called "spooky action at a distance."

On a more mundane scale, realize that staying together can be compared to what happens in the marketplace. As long as both people in a relationship believe that their partner provides a greater value (more affection, freedom, support, or passion—whatever's important to them) than someone else might, they'll remain coupled. Just as the shopper who loves the bargains at Kmart gets lured into Wal-Mart one day for a better deal, or, for that matter, the wine connoisseur who buys a different label instead of the old favorite when another vintner has a stellar year, anyone can be enticed away by the promise of something perceived as "better." Set aside the commercial flavor of this and focus on what I'm telling you: People stay as long as they don't imagine that someone else has something greater to offer. Therefore, they're in their relationships or marriages by default. (I'll explain more about this in the upcoming chapters on values.)

The solution? Instead of daydreaming about eternity, focus on what you can do today to be caring, honor your own and your partner's values, and bring greater perceived fulfillment to both of you.

A couple of years ago while I was in Sydney, Australia, my late wife was sailing in the Mediterranean on one of our homes called *The World,* a luxurious floating city at sea that continually circumnavigates the globe. Upon anchoring just offshore from Portofino, Italy, she took a boat into the port, disembarked, and walked along the water's edge into one of the many designer-shoe boutiques. Moments later, the most handsome man she'd ever laid eyes on entered the store and purchased three expensive pairs of designer shoes. (This, as you can imagine, is generally high on many women's lists of values. Although men may have descended from apes, women most certainly must have come from centipedes— for how else can you explain why they purchase 50 times more pairs of shoes than they have feet?) This handsome fellow approached my wife and said, "My God, you're the most beautiful woman I've ever laid eyes on. Please tell me you're not married."

She, being momentarily stunned by his alluring appearance, said cautiously, "Actually, yes, I am married." He introduced himself and stated that he was originally from Milan and had just arrived in Portofino on a ship owned by a prince of Arabia. He asked if he could please invite her to lunch or dinner, either on the ship or in the port. She said that she couldn't join him, but was certainly grateful for the compliment and was flattered by his invitation.

She rushed back to *The World* and immediately e-mailed me about the meeting. She said that she was truly touched that such a handsome young man in his mid to late 30s found her so attractive. I responded in agreement: that she was truly beautiful and that I could easily see why he was so spellbound. I told her that she deserved such acknowledgment and that if she'd love to enjoy his company, then by all means please feel free to do so. I wrote to her that anything could happen to me as I travel, and that it might be wise to accept such an invitation so that she could rule him in or out, especially since it was a unique and serendipitous meeting.

I felt at the time that she'd make a wise assessment of his overall value, power, and presence. I was aware that each person does a conscious or unconscious evaluation of all relationship prospects relative to the seven areas and powers of life, which you'll learn more about in later chapters. I knew that she'd easily discern his spiritual, mental, vocational, financial, familial, social, and physical powers and standards.

I also knew that if she let the meeting remain as just an alluring fantasy, I'd then be compared to what she imagined him to be like, and I wouldn't fare as well in contrast, particularly since I was more mature in age. If she made a more complete evaluation of him, however, she'd be free to either fulfill her ever-growing aspirations with him or rule him out completely as someone not as fabulous as she might have initially imagined—and I would be appreciated even more in comparison. I felt that I couldn't lose by encouraging her to make such an investigation.

Since she met me in Venice just days later for a romantic rendezvous, I fared well in the competitive market—I might even say with more than normal affection. Only if I were certain in my own power could I encourage such freedom for my lovely wife, thereby honoring her values and providing her an essential power to make decisions. For this she respected me even more and appreciated that she had someone who knew that nothing's missing and that love can never be destroyed, only changed in form.

Myth #4: Once We Get Past These Rough Waters, It Will Be Smooth Sailing

Relationships aren't static, so no one fix eliminates all your supposed troubles. As I've already said, it's human nature to have ups and downs, happiness and sadness, support and challenge, attraction and repulsion, and so on.

Even if you've already embraced this idea, it's still tempting to think that if life gets easier, things with other people will be "better." Not so! **Maximum evolvement occurs at the border of chaos and order.** Therefore, if you ever get everything just so, you end up attracting or creating new confusion just to keep you on the edge, to make things challenging, and to guarantee continued development. Whether you know it consciously or not, you have an undeniable impulse to grow, so you automatically put things in place to ensure that it happens, such as getting involved with someone who will push you in that direction. Remember, the purpose of relationships is to balance your perceptions and to help you perceive, own, and appreciate your own wholeness. This purpose requires periods of difficulty just as much as times of ease. Life involves a balance of each, of liberty and constraint.

Myth #5: A Good Relationship Requires Sacrifice

Simply put, sacrifice breeds resentment. Although some religions glorify acts of selflessness, there's actually no such thing. Ultimately, attempts to annihilate any motive to do well by yourself are futile. This means that any time you do something you don't want to do and don't see any benefit for yourself in doing, you'll resent it, either immediately and consciously or on subconscious levels that will bubble up later, without fail. It looks like this:

- You give something you didn't really want to give.
- You don't get the acknowledgment, reward, or reciprocation that you think you deserve.
- You become disappointed and resentful.
- Then you feel guilty for not being unselfishly generous.
- And finally, you feel the need to sacrifice again.

It can become a self-defeating cycle. I don't care if you're a parent giving to a child, a worker to a company, or a romantic to a lover, this behavior eventually leads to resentment. There's always a hidden agenda of *What's in it for me?* It's often suppressed, and this is why sacrifice is ultimately unwise and incomplete.

Does this mean that there's no such thing as altruism, philanthropy, or generosity? No, it just means that anytime these exist, so do egocentricity, misanthropy, and greed. There's always a balancing force, even if it's sometimes hidden or unconscious. Acknowledging this fact helps you see why it's so important to link what you love with whatever you do, or to simply say no.

The corollary to the myth of necessary sacrifice is the idea that you have to consciously and continually balance give-and-take. The challenge of living with this approach, though, is that your idea of equilibrium is often defined according to your potentially one-sided perceptions and doesn't always recognize a true "fair exchange," since it doesn't always consider all parties' needs or values equally. If you try to make sure that things are always even with your partner or friends, you might wind up keeping an unfair score. As you run such a mental tally, you can start to experience varying degrees of selfishness and stinginess when you feel you've given too much, and grades of guilt and unworthiness when you feel you've taken too much. When you live according to this myth, such a road can, again, lead to resentment.

If instead you can learn to see that there's *already* a perfectly balanced give-and-take in any relationship—that it's just a matter of discerning the forms of exchange that are unique to you and your loved ones—then you can change your perspective entirely. You can begin to see that keeping mental tallies isn't what's important. Instead, it's the ability to articulate and translate what you'd love to receive and bestow in terms of what your partner wants: That's true fair exchange.

What if you could experience what you'd love to have by helping someone else get what they desire? Conversely, what if you could help someone else see how they receive according to their values by giving in alignment with yours? **You could eliminate sacrifice altogether and empower one another to grant each other's heartfelt requests.** There's an art and science to asking in a way that inspires an unreserved *yes,* as well as knowing how to hear requests so that you see how to say *yes* without hesitation. It also helps you get clear on when *no* is the right answer for you so that you can decline without a hidden agenda or brewing resentment—and you can then hear others say *no* with the same equanimity. Again, you'll learn more about how to do this in upcoming chapters.

Myth #6: Great Sex Happens Only at the Beginning of a Relationship

There's no denying that sex for the first time (or first several times) can feel hot, electric, ecstatic, and mind-numbingly, flesh-tinglingly new. I sometimes call it the "mounting reflex," which is in response to the yearning and passion of the sex organs, also known as *lust.*

There's also heart-to-heart, eye-to-eye, light-to-light cocoon love. It's intimate. You get lost in someone else's being; and you stop feeling the separation between your bodies, minds, hearts, and souls. This is no reflex. It's the personal, heart-to-heart *aflex,* a word I made up to describe the free choice to love in the present, in contrast to an automatic response. Let's call this true and intimate lovemaking.

Which one is better: lust or lovemaking, reflex or aflex? Which one would you want to experience for the rest of your days? The good news is that you don't have to choose. These two types of sex can occur at different levels all through your life, even in relationships that last beyond the initial infatuation stage. **Both lust and lovemaking can continue to grow and evolve, as long as you understand and disable the mechanisms that might shut them down.**

These disruptive phenomena amount to letting your fantasies and unrealistic expectations (not necessarily your sexual desires, but the myths I'm describing in this chapter) dictate the relationship. Nothing flips the "off" switch faster than putting up emotional barriers as a result of someone not living up to your unwisely projected expectations. If you don't know how to dissolve those walls, your sexual interest and intensity will predictably dwindle.

By the same token, I've seen the gift of sex resurge, as with one couple I knew who'd been married for 30 years. They dissolved the emotional charges between them and initiated an entirely fresh, grateful, and intimate bond with incredibly satisfying sex. (Later in this book, you'll learn and practice the method that they used to do this.) Soon, you'll discover how both partners can continue to grow sexually for the entire life of the relationship.

Myth #7: In the Right Relationship, I Won't Have to Work at It

This one's almost a no-brainer, although many people hang on to the idea that being with someone should happen "naturally." As you probably already know, at least on an intellectual level, a fulfilling relationship requires concentration, organization, effort, and skill. There's serious work in keeping and developing *any* connection with others, whether it's personal or professional. Think of *work* only as the movement of some force over some distance, as action and energy. Using this definition, it becomes obvious: **Any relationship requires work if it is to live.**

Anytime you don't put action and energy into your relationships, they automatically undergo entropy and decay. Staying close to someone is an uphill process because both people are changing and evolving. If you don't keep up with the other person's value system and your own, and maintain the skills of communicating your preferences in terms of theirs (skills you'll learn in an upcoming chapter), someone else could come along and distract one of you, perhaps permanently.

Myth #8: If I'm Not Involved with Someone, I'll Be Lonely

Have you ever been physically close to someone, even in bed, and felt a huge distance between you? Have you ever been thousands of miles from another person yet felt as if they were right next to you? If so, then you already know that loneliness has little to do with being alone.

Feeling lonesome is more a function of how you perceive yourself relative to your environment. The myth that this problem will be solved by someone else's presence goes back to one we covered earlier, the idea that someone else can "complete" you. Both of these myths come from a common phenomenon that all of us have in varying degrees: not recognizing all parts of ourselves. For some reason, everyone thinks that other people possess qualities they themselves don't—the grass is always greener, so to speak.

In a dependent relationship, you assume that the other person has something you don't. Yet you do have their traits, although possibly in a different form because you have a different hierarchy of values. Honor your own way of being! The next time you meet someone who seems to have something you lack, you'd be wise to look deeper and see where you actually do have it. Keep asking yourself where you possess this attribute until you can see that you own it in equal measure—yes, to the same degree. It completely changes the dynamic of the relationship and erases dependency. Over the last 20 years, I've had the opportunity to watch tens of thousands of people from all over the world make this amazing discovery. It's incredibly powerful and life changing. We're truly mirrors of each other.

When you see that trait in yourself, you suddenly realize that you can share your talents, mutually empowering one another. For example, if your career was to suddenly derail while your spouse was excelling professionally, you might minimize yourself in the relationship if you thought that your partner had something you didn't. You might become addicted to this person and frightened of being left. Yet if you can see where your power is and the form it takes, you can choose to share your strength and enjoy the other person's energy, too. In the coming pages, I'll show you how to awaken conscious awareness of all that you are and all that you have to share.

People often use the illusion of loneliness to stay in an unfulfilling situation, or to jump from one commitment to the next without discrimination. For those who are seemingly alone and buying into this myth, watch out for the number one relationship repellent that this false belief creates: desperation. **Remember, nothing's missing.** You can become aware that you have everything you think a relationship delivers without the other person "giving" it to you. You'll see how as you continue reading.

Myth #9: Children Complete a Marriage

Child rearing has two sides, just like everything else. As a parent, you have one part of you that consciously or unconsciously feels elated and excited, and another part that wonders what on earth you've gotten yourself into. Having a baby is happy and sad right from the beginning.

Clearly, children don't complete a couple any more than romantic partners complete one another. In truth, the most common effect of having kids is for the parents to live vicariously through their offspring, getting to reexperience old pleasure and pain in familiar or novel ways.

At the same time, children tend to express the parents' repressed or disowned parts. For example, if a mother and father are unable to embrace their own sexuality, a child may become promiscuous, horrifying them and forcing them to confront aspects of sexual expression that they've avoided. Or, as another example, if the parents always hold in feelings of anger, the child may rage, giving voice to unspoken fury. I've heard it described as *the plunger effect:* Whatever emotion one person pushes down comes pouring out of someone else who doesn't have the controls screwed on so tight.

Children become a mirror that parents can look into and learn to appreciate. The members of this relationship temper one another and teach each other about the yin and yang of existence. By learning from their kids' behavior, moms and dads can also impart some wisdom about human nature, accelerating the personal evolution of the child.

Studies show that the more educated the culture, the slower its population grows. There are religious exceptions, but in general, this is true. The more socioeconomically depressed a society is, the higher its reproduction rate. As people gain more knowledge, they become more integrated and recognize that they have all parts—they don't need offspring to deliver what's supposedly missing. What's more, they understand a concept I call *childrenomics:* They realize that wealth depends on having fewer children. The educated also tend to live at a higher level on Abraham Maslow's hierarchy of needs, which means that they'll be more interested in such values as personal empowerment (self-actualization) than in the physical perpetuation of the species (survival).

Children foster a feeling of completeness, in that they can feel like an extension of yourself. Are they necessary for that? No. Are they a manifestation of that? Yes. Are there certain things that children can bring to you in awareness and education? Yes and no. Please understand this: No one's missing a mother, father, sister, brother, son, or daughter. Nobody! You'll appreciate and integrate that as we continue. The truth is that everybody has everybody.

Myth #10: Opposites Attract

At this point in your reading, you may be starting to see that you have no real opposite. You may have disowned parts of yourself, which you'll decide to date, marry, or even parent. But make no mistake: **All parts are there inside you, whether you acknowledge them or not.**

It may seem as if opposites attract merely because you don't see yourself in someone else right away. You get infatuated with parts of them that you think are special and theirs alone, and you can't see that you have them, too. When you do this, you unconsciously filter out anything that goes against your values and exaggerate whatever you consider more supportive or positive.

Later, when friction starts to develop because of perceived differences, you again deny that what bugs you, turns you off, and drives you crazy also resides in you in equal measure but in a different form. The other person appears not to support your values, so now that's making you nuts. When your partner begins challenging you, you may think, *I don't want to be in this relationship!* That's because your unawakened self, that part of you living in the fantasy of having pleasure without pain, positive without negative, is attracted to whatever you think is similar to you or what you believe supports your highest values.

Psychologist Carl Jung observed, "Everything that irritates us about others can lead us to an understanding of ourselves." When someone starts to get on your nerves, that's your opportunity, again, to look inside and find that very same trait in yourself—and discover that you have it in equal measure. This could be described as claiming your disowned parts, and it's when you experience a personal growth spurt in your relationship. Indeed, the universe is designed to assure your growth, so you attract and are drawn to people who *appear* to be your opposite, and as a result, you get a balance of like and dislike, support and challenge.

Just to drive this point home, let's imagine that you meet someone and go out on a date. You project onto him or her an ideal of more positives than negatives, imagining that this person supports you more than challenges you. You like this person and you're infatuated. You start seeing all the things in him or her that are similar to you: "Oh, you have two eyes! So do I! How many ribs do you have? The same number as I do! We must be soul mates! Look . . . you have skin! And two nostrils!" All right, I'm being facetious, but you definitely identify the similarities and exaggerate them and their importance. *Infatuation,* **according to the Greeks, was an exaggeration of similarities.** *Resentment* **is an exaggeration of differences.** *Love* **is equally embracing both.**

Once you've lived through the infatuation stage, and the other person doesn't live up to the fantasy, you resent him or her. Guess what you say: "We don't have a thing in common. We don't see eye to eye anymore. We have two different lives, and we don't get along. We just don't have the same goals."

When you first engage in a relationship with someone, you tend to put that individual on a pedestal and minimize yourself. You feel as if you can't live without him or her, and you want to hurry up and be together. That's conditional infatuation, not love. When the person doesn't live up to your fantasy, you realize you've been gullible; and you get angry because you were foolish enough to project your values and therefore unrealistic expectations onto him or her. You notice all the differences while becoming blind to the similarities, and you start punishing the other person.

Anybody whom you praise, you'll also reprimand. If you elevate someone on a pedestal, you'll also banish the person into a pit. It would be wiser to put people into your heart, wouldn't it? Nobody deserves the pedestal or the pit, and everybody is worth caring for. Yes, everybody!

Breaking Free of the Myths

Just reading the words in this chapter—even if you see their wisdom right away—won't immediately and completely detach the hold that myths may have on you. That's why, at the end of this and every chapter throughout this book, I've included exercises that will help you integrate these ideas and make them seem even more real to you than the fairy-tale fantasies.

Do these exercises as you go along. You don't need to finish the entire book right away—but do begin the exercises as soon as you turn the last page of each chapter. If there's a daily application, add the item(s) to your calendar so that you have a reminder, and take at least one action toward completion right away. You'll find the rewards nearly immediate in helping you create more fulfilling, more real, and (if you'd love to have them) lasting relationships.

Actions to Create More Fulfilling Relationships

— **Keep a notebook.** Get a loose-leaf binder, purchase a blank journal, or set up a file on your computer to make notes about what you're learning. Notice whenever any of the myths show up as fantasies that you're projecting onto someone else. Step back and see how the Words of Power (explained in the following paragraph) can effectively assist you in creating the kind of personal and professional relationships you'd love to have in your life.

— **Integrate the Words of Power.** Here's an exercise that I created for my book *You Can Have an Amazing Life . . . in Just 60 Days!* It's based on an affirmation technique I devised when I was transforming myself from being a surf bum and high school dropout to living the life of my dreams, with abundant wealth in all areas—spiritual, mental, career, finances, family, social, and physical. I've found no other method more powerful than this for changing false beliefs (fantasies) into more empowering expectations for myself and what I can truly create, so I've included some Words of Power at the end of every chapter for you. Try this:

1. Read the Words of Power out loud seven times. Unlike some affirmations, they're not lopsided promises of happily ever after. They're balanced, inspiring statements of true possibilities—the opposite of the myths addressed in this chapter—that call you to live more profoundly in their presence.

Words of Power

My relationships move me toward a greater appreciation and understanding of my own wholeness.

Nothing is missing in me. I am complete unto myself.

I am the same in essence—though different in existence—as all others, and it is primarily or only my hierarchy of values that distinguishes me.

I embrace the truth that love has a balance of support and challenge.

I am surrounded by love 24 hours a day.

No matter what I have done or not done, I am worthy of love.

2. Create your own Words of Power using your own language and any phrases that inspire you from the chapter you've just read. Write them in your notebook and then repeat them seven times.

3. Take a few moments to reflect on what you've read; and in your notebook, record any insights that come to you.

4. For 21 days, repeat the Words of Power (both those I've listed and the ones you've written yourself) seven times each day, ideally either at night as you're falling asleep or first thing in the morning as you wake up.

�✳✳ ✳✳✳

CHAPTER TWO

Giving Up the Fantasy in Favor of Fulfillment

If only we'd stop trying to be happy,
we could have a pretty good time.
— Edith Wharton

This often-quoted phrase is generally thought to be cynical, but if you give it a moment to sink in, you can see its wisdom, too. Wharton could simply be telling us that in our endless pursuit of one-sidedness, we're denying ourselves fulfillment.

If you're ready to let go of the dream of loved ones who don't have so-called flaws, then you're ready for something even greater than the fantasy: fulfillment.

This means you're willing to stop imagining that you'll parent idealized kids who are independent . . . yet always considerate, kind, and obedient. You'll quit expecting a lover to be constantly sexy, turned on, and available (never tired, irritable, or uninterested). You'll no longer cling to the idea of the mythical spouse who's only loyal, supportive, and nonjudgmental. You'll give up hoping that your parents will turn into some contemporary version of Ozzie and Harriet Nelson—or Ozzy and Sharon Osbourne, or whatever fantasy couple you hold up as a paragon of parental virtue.

In essence, fulfillment comes from appreciating both sides, happiness and sadness—everything that you or society has misidentified as "good" and "bad." It comes from observing your own illusions, acknowledging that your own perceptions create your experiences, and being willing to look beyond this to recognize what you and everyone else are really seeking . . . which is love. Seeking fulfillment means looking for love. Yet, as the Zen masters assure us, there's no search to be done. You must simply wake up and see what you already have and who you are.

All of us are expressions of love. We're also independent and dependent, kind and cruel, obedient and unruly, and so on. No one has only positive traits; and the minute you start wishing for someone who does, or start believing that's what you or another person should be, you're living in a fantasy. But when you start loving whatever parts of yourself you've previously disowned, then you can embrace them in the world, too.

As you read and complete the exercises in this book, you'll learn to see that every person is "both/and," not "either/or." This can be profoundly challenging, especially when someone comes along and starts pushing your buttons. Those individuals offer incredible gifts, though. Whatever irritates you about them—their behavior, speech, beliefs, or anything else—is the *very thing* you can learn to identify and then embrace in yourself. Button pushers point the way to those parts of yourself that you've disowned.

What kind of relationships might you expect if you relinquish your fantasies as well as their converse nightmares? What could happen if you start acknowledging that your disowned self shows up again and again in the mirror of your relationships? If you're no longer trying to make other people happy, and you're not counting on them to do the same for you, then what will your interactions be about?

Here are some things to look for:

- You can expect new illusions to crop up. **It's one of the fascinating parts of being human: our insatiable appetite and capacity for fantasy.** You just create a different one, a new facet to peer through in the prism of love. You'll constantly be challenged by new things in order to learn about yourself and how you relate to others.

- You gain a greater understanding of yourself as you integrate more and more of your disowned parts, what Jungian psychologists call the *shadow*. As you shine light on it, you begin to recognize its value in your life. You don't just accept it, saying, "Oh, well, I guess I'm not perfect." No! **You start to see how the shadow self is part of the perfection.** You see the gifts of these previously unappreciated aspects of yourself. This is what I mean when I say that relationships awaken you to the inherent balance existing within and around you and assist you in acknowledging your own magnificence and wholeness.

- When you stop projecting your fantasies onto others, you're able to more clearly see and appreciate people for who they are. You notice whenever you're setting up unrealistic expectations and choose something different: You can go to what you know about the person's ideals and base your hopes on that. **The only reasonable expectation you can have of people is that they will live according to their values.**

That last point, in a nutshell, tells you why it's critical to understand what's important to the people who are close to you. Obviously, you can't control or predict a person's every move, and who would want to, anyway? But, living in the practical world, you'll expect certain things.

For example, one of my male clients employs a chief assistant who values her family a bit more than the work she does for him. So he can expect—based on that value—that if she has to choose between being there for her daughter in some important way and being at work to help him do his business, she's going to pick her little girl almost every time. This doesn't mean that she does a poor job at work—on the contrary, she's a wonderfully dedicated, productive, and highly skilled colleague, and a delightful person to boot. This is also because she can see how her job is helping her family. My client appreciates knowing what's most important to his employee because he can make his decisions and plans—as well as communicate with her—in a more effective way. He now speaks to her in a manner that relates to what's actually going on in her life and what's truly important to her, not only what he fantasizes that she "ought" to be doing.

Similarly, I know that travel is something that's important to my partner, Starr. Because this is a high priority for me, too, this means we get to spend a lovely bit of time together. It would be unreasonable for me to expect someone who prefers being at home to want to meet me all over the world.

The *only* assurance you have about whether your expectations are reasonable is knowing someone's values. What's more, people will show you love through *their* perspective—not always through yours. When you expect them to live primarily according to your beliefs or in line with unrealistic social norms, you'll probably feel unloved.

If your father's highest values are education, business, and finance, he'll show you his love by supporting you when you learn, work, or save; and he'll challenge you when you do almost anything else. If your mother treasures family, social relationships, health, and beauty, she'll show you her affection by supporting you when you're getting along with your relatives, interacting well with your friends, and when you're feeling and looking your best. She'll resist you when you defy or neglect these same actions. Knowing your own and your loved ones' ideals is crucial so that you can feel their affection and not imagine that it doesn't exist just because it gets expressed according to a system other than your own.

What's Important to You?

Every individual, regardless of race, creed, color, sex, or age, inherently has a set of values. We each have something we think is most important, second most important, third most important, and so on. We call this set of priorities a *hierarchy of values*. Our individual hierarchies determine how we sense the world, filter those perceptions, and interpret and react to what we feel and think as a result.

Imagine a husband and wife. Her highest values are raising her children, educating them, and safeguarding the health of her family; while his are making money, building resources and business, and providing for his family. (I don't mean to reinforce stereotypes here, but we'll explore this scenario since it's so common.) Imagine this couple shopping, walking hand in hand. As they stroll the plaza, she sees things that he doesn't, and vice versa.

She spots toys for the kids, school clothes, books and games that will help her children learn, healthy snacks, and brochures for family activities—all kinds of items that align with her values. She'll notice and filter her vision through her unique set of principles. Her husband will walk through the plaza and see none of those things; in fact, his eyes will avoid them. He'll notice *The Wall Street Journal,* computers, books and magazines for entrepreneurs, and gifts for clients—anything that might help him in business or in his intellectual development, because those things matter to him.

The *hierarchy of their values*—not gender or anything else—determines how they filter their reality and their environment; they see opportunities accordingly. What they realize through their senses is their reality, which is determined by the beliefs they project.

I'll repeat: **All human beings act according to their own values!** Write that in your heart, because it's an important principle. We often project our system onto other people, expecting them to adhere to it, rather than honoring them as they act in line with their own.

Anytime you expect someone to live outside of their own value system, you create a false expectation. However, you can choose to learn the art of communicating your priorities in terms of theirs. In direct proportion to how well you can do that, they'll still live according to their beliefs, but in a way that satisfies both of you.

For example, Mary and Todd are deciding whether to buy a new car. Mary says, "Yes, we need a new car because the one we have is outdated, and we can afford a new one. Besides, we deserve to treat ourselves because we both work so hard."

Todd says, "No—what about our retirement fund?" He thinks that a down payment and raised insurance rates, plus the monthly payments, will cut too sharply into their ability to save.

After Mary gives this some thought, she figures out a way to give Todd what he'd love while getting what she wants, too: She estimates how much they've been spending on maintenance and fuel (the old car is a gas-guzzling SUV) and shows him how that would be offset when they purchase a two-year-old, "gently used" but fuel-efficient car. She points out that their insurance premium would stay about the same, and they can put down cash for more than half of the purchase price and pay off the rest in a little more than a year. They can recoup their investment in just under two years with the savings on gas and maintenance.

With this plan, both people's desires are more fully honored and understood. Taking the time to consider and communicate our own values in terms of others' pays many dividends!

Resistance Is Futile

There's a funny off-Broadway musical called *I Love You, You're Perfect, Now Change.* Sound familiar? Have you ever thought you've found the perfect mate and then spent the rest of your relationship together trying to "fix" him or her? Futile, isn't it?

The moment you project onto other people and expect them to live according to your values instead of their own, you label them as "bad" (or some version of that, such as a judgmental "lazy," "sloppy," or "rude"). You think they need to be changed, and you're just the one to do it. After all, you're the one with the "right" values . . . aren't you?

Maybe you're starting to think that all you have to do is find someone with the exact same belief system as you and then everything will be just peachy. I've done my research, and I can assure you that no two people ever have the exact same priorities—they're as unique as fingerprints or voices. We can compare this to a principle in physics called the *Pauli exclusion principle:* No two quantum particles, or people, will ever have the same quantum numbers or representation of the universe.

That poses a challenge for relationships, doesn't it? Everyone sees through different eyes, and we still must interact with others who have totally different expectations. As if that's not tough enough, we then compound it with something else.

If Joe attempts to live in line with some idealism that society, his culture, or his family may have imposed, he'll be uncertain of his actual values. He'll act as he "should" instead of being himself. If he then meets Carol and becomes infatuated, he'll put her on a pedestal. He'll assume that she has her life put together better than he does, and he'll think that somehow his values are wrong and hers are right.

Have you ever done this—questioned yourself and started trying to change to please someone else? When you idolize someone, you tend to inject their beliefs into yours. Then you find yourself thinking, *I really ought to be doing this. I should do that. I'm supposed to do this.* You try to live by someone else's system, but still have your own, creating internal conflict. You live with moral dilemmas and imperatives.

Perhaps instead of putting someone on a pedestal with infatuation, you put someone in a pit with resentment. As another example, let's say you're walking down the street and spot a homeless person, avoiding him, and thinking he's less than you are. You minimize him, rather than exaggerate him. Instead of injecting his value system into yours, you force your judgment onto him. You think, *He ought to get a job. He shouldn't be asking me for money. He's supposed to contribute more to society!* You don't see him for who he ultimately is and the service he contributes.

How often have you done this sort of thing? As long as you're "shoulding" on yourself with others' ideas, or "shoulding" on others with your own, you're spending futile energy.

The hierarchy of your values dictates your destiny. Trying to live someone else's way or imposing yours on others is patently unwise. Ralph Waldo Emerson once said, "Envy is ignorance . . . [and] imitation is suicide." Yet most everyone does both—in fact, our society encourages it. The media machine commonly chooses heroes to idealize, and the public accepts those individuals' into their own lives. Of course, when the heroes have their inevitable falls from grace, we throw them into the pit, at least for a while.

Higher and Lower Order

You, like every other human, focus on what's most important to you. Therefore, whatever's highest in your values hierarchy will also have the most order (that is, steady, concentrated focus and a surplus of attention). Chaos increases as you go down the list (that is, unsteady, scattered focus, approaching attention deficit disorder).

Returning to our previous example of the husband and wife, this means that if the wife's highest values are her children, their health, and her home, she has that organized. But forget about her profession, finances, and everything else—unless she has them connected to her real priorities. She may not know how to keep and balance a checkbook or run a business. It would be chaotic if you put her in charge of a sales and promotion campaign for your business—yet she might excel if you gave her the task of fund-raising for her children's school. On the other hand, if the husband has business and finance as his top priorities, that's where you'll find his order and organization. But if you put him in front of a bunch of kids, he's lost and helpless—chaos! That is, until you have him in an elementary classroom to do market research on a new product he's developing for that age-group.

Your hierarchy of values determines which parts of your life are ordered and which parts are chaotic, where you're disciplined and where you aren't. You always make time for what's high on your list but never seem to have time for things that are lower. That's why, when one spouse says, "Honey, I want you to do this (thing that the other spouse isn't interested in) . . ." the other person says, "Yeah, yeah, yeah . . ." and never gets around to doing it—because it isn't high on their values ladder. It simply isn't a priority. Those who say yes but then don't follow through could be perceived as delaying, procrastinating, and being uncooperative; but if they were able to see how following through would actually support what's important to them, they'd get right on it. Then they could be perceived as extremely disciplined and devoted. Either way, people always act with absolute faithfulness to their own values. Can you see this in your own life?

Here's an example of how this worked with a young man I met in Los Angeles. His father was a consulting client of mine, an exceedingly respected financier who came from a prominent family. The father asked me to work with his son because, he said, the 19-year-old was lazy, unmotivated, undisciplined, and was doing poorly in school—he was just sitting around doing nothing. Although I suggested that maybe there was something to be done about this on the father's end (since it was evident that this was pushing his buttons), he said that he was too busy and that his son would meet me in my hotel room.

When I met the young man, I immediately found out where he was spending his time and energy. Based on how much "order" was in this area, it was clear that the most important things in his value system were girls and certain activities with them.

Every evening, the father would come home after a long day at work and see his son getting ready for a night of partying. The father would think, *He shouldn't be going out. He should be staying home and studying to bring up his grades!* The boy would disappear for the night, and then when Dad got up early to go to work, he would see his son sleeping in. Now he'd really start projecting: *He's lazy! His grades are no good! Nothing gets him up!*

What the father didn't realize was that when the son came home at two or three in the morning, the older man was asleep. From this young person's perspective, the father was wasting his life, and vice versa.

Who was "right"? Remember, the son spent six hours of due diligence picking up girls. Focused! Nonstop! This was heavy-duty action! Meanwhile, the father stifled his own sexuality at home; and the son acted out the family dynamic, expressing a repression. What's more, the father gave his son a large allowance every month, so it wasn't necessary for him to earn his own money, yet they fought about his not working.

The truth is, the son was dedicated to his highest purpose—his mission—and he was focused. He was disciplined in his most significant values. I don't know about you, but spending six hours each night on the sole objective of picking up a girl seems like a lot of dedication and hard work to me! I know I'd be burned out trying to keep up that schedule.

The son said he wanted to do well in school, but he just wasn't motivated. I showed him how excelling in his course work could help his social life. I asked him, "Do you think girls would prefer to have men who are intelligent or stupid?"

He said, "Probably intelligent."

"Do you think they'd rather be with somebody who's doing well and has money, or someone who's broke?"

He replied, "Probably the one with the cash."

I asked, "Do you think that a person who's going to work, being diligent, and earning would be likely to have a higher selection of girls?"

The light went on: "Yeah!"

I spent about three hours with him, linking every class he was taking to—in his words—*picking up chicks*. Associating: class—chicks. Math, science, economics, business management —chicks!

In the next three months, his grades skyrocketed, and he also discovered something he thought was really useful. According to him, there were two types of girls: (1) those who, if he was confident and excelled in school, were attracted to him (daughterlike figures), and (2) ones who, if he was humble and asked for their help in studying, were attracted to him (motherlike figures). Either way, he was getting what he wanted most.

Obviously, he *was* disciplined, according to *his* values and not his father's. If someone projected their ideas onto him and labeled him lazy, it wasn't much different from condemning a child with attention deficit disorder when the same child will sit and watch a video game for six hours straight. Such a person will stay completely focused, memorize every single player and strategy, and compete at the game nonstop with a buddy. These children have highly concentrated value systems, but to reach them, others must be willing to learn what that hierarchy is and relate to them based on it, not their own.

I frequently give presentations to teenagers and share my life story with them. I tell them about being born with several physical challenges and being labeled a slow learner who would never read, write, or communicate well. I talk about how I compensated by excelling at sports, but then moved to a new school where I was frequently used as my classmates' punching bag. I describe leaving home at 14 to become a surf bum, nearly dying of strychnine poisoning at 17, discovering my mission and purpose in life later that year, and so on. I own up to being interested in the same kinds of things that they're into right now, some of which don't earn parental approval. There are often moments when this supposedly cynical audience of teenagers is in tears: Their hearts open wide. They get inspired, and so do their teachers. For just a moment, you can sense that. After I finish speaking, I open the floor to questions, and many students put their hands up because they're engaged, curious, and want to participate.

Afterward, teachers often come to me and say, "We've never seen such a thing! We usually have disruptions. These kids are aggravating, cause problems, talk, and don't pay attention!"

I usually tell them, "The difference is that I found and linked to their values and communicated in those terms; and as a result, they were with me. They were present. The things you talk to them about and project onto them . . . you're not trying to find out their beliefs and communicate in terms of their value systems."

This happens all over the world, wherever I go. That's because the phenomenon of people projecting onto others happens *everywhere*. In schools, you get to see a microcosm of the world. Those children want to learn! But they don't want to do so with coercion and judgment: The art is to learn how to communicate what you want to teach them in terms of what matters to them.

There are no lazy people, difficult people, know-it-alls, snobs, or bums! These are just labels. In actuality, everyone has these traits and their opposite traits, and they're just expressed in different forms based on one's beliefs.

Soon you'll learn in greater detail how you can communicate in terms of someone else's values. This helps others feel understood and loved for who they are, not for who you think they ought to be. **Fulfillment can only occur when you are free and clear to live what is true for you.** Allow others to do that, celebrate their priorities with them, and you'll feel it, too.

Careless, Careful, Caring

If you're exaggerating your value system by self-righteously minimizing someone else's, how does that person probably feel? Angry? Hurt? Both? And what do you find yourself thinking? It's probably something like this: *You should be doing it differently. You ought to be doing that. I want you to do this!* This kind of interaction defines a *careless* relationship. You literally care less about that person and his or her beliefs than you do about yourself and yours, and you project your values. This leads to distance, alienation, and resentment.

What if your mate's actions humble you? Perhaps he or she does something spectacular at work or offers to take care of the entire family for a week so that you can get a break. On the other hand, suppose your partner runs off with someone else. You get down off your self-righteous horse and put yourself down in the dirt. You become "self-wrongeous": You minimize yourself and exaggerate your mate as you walk on eggshells, negating your values and paying attention to the other person's. Now you're creating a *careful* relationship, which leads to misperceptions of sacrifice and resentment.

When you both decide that you'll communicate your priorities in terms of the other person's, you become *caring*. If you're interested in long-term relationships, know that this is what keeps the ring on the finger. In this situation, both people's principles are honored, affirmed, and fulfilled.

Incidentally, what we call *caring* in a personal context is called *selling* in business. To develop quality connections with others, you'll be required to master the art of conveying your values in terms of someone else's in order to demonstrate your affection in this specific way.

Instead of imagining your life with the so-called perfect kids, lover, spouse, boss, parents, friends, and so on, learn to appreciate each of these people for what they bring to you, and get to know their values. In the next chapter, you'll learn how to identify your own and others' values and take the first steps to creating the fulfilling relationships you desire and deserve.

Actions to Create More Fulfilling Relationships

— **Ask yourself a few key questions.** Get out your notebook and make some notes for yourself. Take a look at each of your most important relationships, including your romantic interest(s), friends, family, and colleagues. For each person, ask yourself:

- What unrealistic ideals do I have? Which of my values am I projecting? What *shoulds* and *ought tos* am I giving them, either in my own mind or out loud?

- What drawbacks can I see to that so-called ideal? What negatives would I potentially experience if this person suddenly conformed to my values?

- What benefits can I see in the situation as it is right now? What or how does this person contribute to my life just as he or she is at the moment?

— **Explore your thoughts and feelings about the family in which you grew up.** In your notebook, write the answers to the following questions:

- Who would I be if I had different parents?

- What kind of mom and dad would I have preferred?

- What are the benefits to me of having the parents I had?

- What might be the drawback to me if I had the ones I preferred?

Words of Power

When I see both sides, I experience the heart of love.

Those I unwisely believe to irritate me actually teach me about myself.

My shadow self is part of my perfection.

I expect people to live according to their values, not mine.

When I love others as they are, they become what I love.

※※※ ※※※

CHAPTER THREE

Climbing the Tower: The Values Hierarchy

He who knows others is wise.
He who knows himself is enlightened.
— From the Tao Te Ching

Wouldn't it be useful to be able to tell someone what's really important to you, or even better, to know it for yourself? Not what you think "should" be significant based on your upbringing and the culture in which you now live, but what's actually essential and fulfilling to *you?* Suppose you could realize your key values hierarchy just by looking at your habitual actions and thoughts with fresh eyes?

You can! Values aren't mysterious, and they don't play hide-and-seek. They're as plain as day in your home, office, and car—everywhere you live your life.

Despite this, most people have no idea what's really important to them. I've met many individuals who profess certain values but whose actions demonstrate something altogether different. In the majority of cases, it's not a matter of deliberate deception, but more a result of their distorted perceptions of what's real for them. They've been so influenced about what their value system "ought" to be that they have no idea what it actually is.

Not so long ago, I met an accomplished surgeon who had recently given birth to twins. She was attempting to be supermom: be there for the boys 24/7 and orchestrate lots of family activities and playdates, keep up her own fitness, take care of the house and all the meals, and more. Whether you think this sounds like a delightful ambition or a terrible burden, your reaction is based on your values. It was making this woman crazy, and she was ready to explode.

This new mom sensed emotions that she was ashamed to admit: anger and frustration. She thought that she needed to get a better handle on her feelings to smooth everything over, and she believed that her husband needed to step up to the plate and help out at home.

When we started talking about her priorities, though, it became apparent that the solution wasn't some new psychological tool for herself or to "fix" her husband. Instead, she needed clarity about the kind of life she would really love for herself. What she'd created wasn't fulfilling her and had little chance of ever doing so because it did nothing to honor her highest value. By taking on the challenging roles of mom and homemaker to the exclusion of everything else, she began to feel that she'd "sacrificed" what was most important to her: developing and practicing her skill as a surgeon who saved lives.

This wasn't easy for her to admit. After all, she lives in a society that, for all its bluster about equality, still deems women who don't put family first as somehow cold, masculine, or otherwise deficient. She resisted for a long while, bursting into tears, berating herself for being selfish, and sheepishly questioning whether it was okay for her to feel this way.

In the end, she was courageous enough to acknowledge the truth: Although she adored her children, raising her family was a value that ranked slightly below her professional calling. She recognized that it was difficult for her husband to help her in any meaningful way and that she was projecting a fantasy—"shoulding" on him. In fact, because she wasn't earning her previously generous salary, her husband had to spend extra time at work to make up some of the gap in their income, and he constantly came home exhausted.

She decided to make some changes: to carefully select someone who could help with child care, to hire additional assistance around the house, and to resume a part-time schedule at the hospital. Her $1,000-an-hour compensation would more than pay for these new services, ease the financial burden so that her husband wouldn't have to work so much, and help her experience the fulfillment she craved.

She also determined that she'd be careful not to let the hospital run her life the way it had in her younger days because that would impinge on her time with family, starting a different cycle of dissatisfaction and unfulfilled goals. Instead, she decided to allot her time *according to her values,* and the relief she felt just from making this decision was immediate.

Being consciously aware of your own belief system simplifies many aspects of your life. If you're clear on what's important to you, previously murky ethical dilemmas get sorted out fairly quickly. You become a more integrated person and expand your perspective, and you even find it easier to appreciate and love others.

If you truly know yourself, then your mission becomes less puzzling, less variable, and more stable. That's because your purpose is revealed at the pinnacle of your values hierarchy. To understand this, imagine your soul above you, with its limitlessness and united consciousness, and then visualize your mind below, with its self-righteous and self-wrongeous illusions. As you look down from your soul's perspective, what does your mind seek to fulfill? What is the "void" that it perceives, and what does it hunger to taste again and again?

A sense of emptiness is the belief that you're missing something or someone, and you give importance to the assumption that you can be satisfied if you fill your perceived void. That's what I mean when I say that voids determine values. **Since nothing is truly missing, both are illusions of the physical senses.** But these illusions are part of the journey of learning to love and being grateful for what is, as it is.

For example, when you feel or believe that you're missing a relationship, you revere and search for one. Whatever's thought to be lacking becomes important, yet everything you're looking for is already present—you're just not recognizing it. When you come to acknowledge, honor, and appreciate the form that it's in, you have the power to transform it into something you love. When you realize that you already have what you desire, you can convert it into new forms. But when you act like you don't have it, it further evades you.

Any perceived void is a point of disconnection with the divine, God, or the universe—whatever you choose to call it. You feel that you can't get enough, although in the realm of spirit, there's always plenty. Nothing is missing. On a higher level, you experience what your soul already is: overflowing and abundant through its communion with infinite supply. That's why, when you're consciously living according to your highest values and not fighting them, you feel so expanded and fulfilled. In that moment, for just an instant, your hierarchy dissolves and nothing feels missing.

The more you link all areas of your life and all everyday

tasks to your dearest values (purpose), the more meaningful and fulfilling your life becomes. When you see how whatever you do is connected to your mission, you begin to love what you do—and therefore, do what you love. If you have any "undelegatable" daily action that you're not inspired about, yet you know you're going to do it anyway, find ways to bridge it to your most significant goals—and watch your vitality grow and your goal become even more alive.

Ask yourself, *How specifically does this action help me fulfill my highest values and purpose?* Don't stop answering this question until you're grateful for having the opportunity to do the action and can feel the resultant surge of energy.

Understanding your own values opens up a greater possibility of creating fulfilling, long-lasting relationships. Keep reading, and you'll discover how to communicate in a way that links your ideals with others', which is the single most important skill in developing, maintaining, and enriching your relationships.

Before you begin linking a previously uninspiring activity to your purpose, or connecting your goals with someone else's, *you must start by identifying your own values,* which are unique to you. The core beliefs you hold and their hierarchy or ranking influence how you perceive (selectively attend to) and how you act in (selectively intend upon) your world. They also, therefore, determine the results you produce and, ultimately, the course of your life.

Your values will tend to express themselves in some or all of seven areas of life: *spiritual, mental, vocational, financial, familial, social,* and *physical.* Each is equally valid as an avenue for a deeply fulfilling connection with the universe. In my experience, about 75 percent of men tend to value mental, financial, and vocational, while about

75 percent of women tend to focus on familial, social, and physical. Twenty-five percent of men focus on the areas more common to women, and vice versa.

Sometimes people allow their fears to keep them from living according to their priorities, and this can cause stress and a sense of emptiness. Understand, though, that even in that case, the values are still running the show. For fun, I call this *the law of lesser pissers:* You'll always choose to "piss off" the person who supports your ideals less. So fear, or avoiding the "greater pisser," is actually an expression of a value, too.

There are seven basic fears that can run your life and keep you from living your life to the fullest:

1. Fear of breaking away from the system of a perceived spiritual authority. *(I don't want to be considered a bad person or go to hell.)*

2. Fear of not having enough mental capability. *(I'm not smart enough. I don't have the credentials or degree.)*

3. Fear of failure. *(I'll fall short.)*

4. Fear of losing it all financially. *(I'll go broke or bankrupt. I won't make enough money to survive.)*

5. Fear of losing loved ones. (*My parents might disown me, my lover will leave me, or my kids will hate me. . . .)*

6. Fear of societal rejection. *(I'm afraid of what everyone will think, I won't fit in, and people won't want to be with me.)*

7. Fear of not having physical capability. *(I'm not tall enough, strong enough, or good-looking enough. I don't have the energy for all this.)*

If, for example, someone's been brought up with a form of religious indoctrination, even if that person has left the organized practice of that faith, the residue of those values remains; and former followers may hesitate to put their full personal hierarchy ahead of the old ways. This fear might reflect such notions as spirituality (as it's been narrowly defined), connection, or acceptance. I constantly meet people who desire wealth but are held back by a spiritual counter-value coupled with an ingrained belief that *money's the root of all evil,* or it's "dirty," and so on. So they're experiencing a conflict of values: material wealth versus religious codes about affluence.

It's important to remember that fear is the result of an unbalanced perspective. You can use what you'll learn later in this book to help you dissolve or collapse whatever concerns you have; but for now, let's just get clear on what you'd really love in your life and acknowledge any areas of apprehension that exist. Internal conflicts are common, but you can ferret out your true self by looking at your life in a particular way. Your values system will become evident as you answer 12 simple questions:

1. How do you fill your space?
2. How do you spend your time?
3. How do you spend your energy?
4. How do you spend your money?
5. Where are you most organized?
6. Where are you most disciplined?

7.   What do you think about?
8.   What do you visualize?
9.   What do you talk to yourself about?
10. What do you speak about with others?
11. What do you react to?
12. What are your goals?

Let's take a look at each of these in turn and see how they all fit together, like puzzle pieces, to answer the most important question: What are *your* values?

1. How Do You Fill Your Space?

As the ancient Greeks asserted, nature abhors a vacuum—and, I'll add, so do values. Take a look at your office, car, home, and wherever you hang out. What have you filled these places with? What objects mean the most to you?

If you enter one of my spaces, wherever that may be, you'll find that it's piled with books and research materials. If you'd peeked into my surgeon friend's home, you'd have seen her diplomas, medical reference books galore, and her collection of antique surgical instruments—all displaced from her office and newly hung in her family room so that she could stay connected with them.

Really look at the places where you spend the most time as if you've never been there before, identifying themes and common elements, which are evidence of your values. Whatever's prevalent in your living, working, and recreational spaces gives you your first clue.

How do you interpret these hints? For the surgeon, the correlation between the objects and her values was pretty obvious. In my case, the subjects of my books and research materials point to my top priority, which is developing my understanding of order in the universe. I pursue and fulfill this by studying biomechanics, economics, sociology, psychology, neuroscience, quantum physics, philosophy, and many other disciplines. The physical evidence of this constant quest is the trail of books and papers I leave wherever I go. The value it represents isn't the accumulation of these physical objects; it's the acquisition of greater wisdom about creation and the cosmos—the big questions.

Think figuratively: A home filled with photos doesn't necessarily mean an appreciation of photography. (What's pictured? Is there a theme?) A home overflowing with flowers might not indicate a love of gardening—maybe it's a connection with the natural world, or possibly a broader desire for beauty. Ask yourself, *What do these things that I've chosen to surround myself with mean to me?*

2. How Do You Spend Your Time?

Often, someone will tell me, "I already know what my highest value is: It's family."

I'll usually get another story when I ask, "How do you spend the 24 hours of each day?" It will go something like this: an hour in the morning at the gym, 14 hours a day at work, an hour or so with the kids and spouse having dinner, a couple hours in the study checking e-mail, and about 6 hours sleeping.

Clearly, this behavior doesn't support the initial claim, even if working 14 hours a day may indicate a profound dedication to being "a good provider" for the family. If people tell me that their highest value is one thing when it's really another, it's usually because *they think they ought to be different.* (Perhaps some authority with that particular belief told them that?) Instead of judging yourself for cherishing something to a different degree than someone else does, learn to recognize that your ideals are just as valid, real, and important as anyone else's.

Also realize that just because something isn't your highest value doesn't mean that it's worth nothing to you. It's completely possible that this 14-hour-a-day worker bee does care for family; it's just not at the top of the hierarchy.

Take a look at how you allocate your waking hours. What claims most of your day? What comes in second? Third? Fourth? The list may not identically parallel your main concerns, but it will come close. To return to our example, here's what that schedule would tell us:

- *Most time:* professional success, earning money (14 hours at work)

- *Second most:* staying connected with people/social (2 hours sending e-mail)

- *Third most/tied:* family (1 hour having dinner with spouse and kids)

- *Third most/tied:* health (1 hour exercising)

Your time is only one indicator, which you can combine with all the others as you do your detective work in figuring out your highest goals. In other words, if you look at your prioritization according to time and view it in consideration of the seven categories coming up, then your values begin to come into sharp focus.

Note: It's possible that your time isn't being spent in support of your beliefs, and this is when conflicts are most often played out. The surgeon/new mom had arranged her life without allotting any of her time to her core value—and that's why she was so stressed. Instead of living according to her own hierarchy, she'd allowed a social norm (such as being acknowledged or respected by others) to take over and reorder her life. If you have the sense that you've done something similar by structuring your days around your idea of what someone else thinks your values *should* be or designing your life around one of the seven fears I outlined earlier, then ask yourself, *How would I spend my time if I believed I had complete choice about it?*

3. How Do You Spend Your Energy?

You'll find clues as to how your hierarchy is stacked by looking at the following characteristics, which are a direct result of where and how you spend your energy:

- You certainly have plenty of energy to do those actions you truly value most, because doing what you love energizes you.

- You clearly become fatigued easily when you can't see how what you're doing will fulfill your highest values. Doing X, Y, and Z rather than A, B, and C on your daily priorities drains you.

Ask yourself, *What actions do I seem to have plenty of energy for? What activities invigorate me? Where do I love to spend the most effort during the day, week, or month?*

You'll require less sleep and express more life force and vigor when you're doing what you love and loving what you do—acting in accordance with what's truly most important to you.

4. How Do You Spend Your Money?

Alfred Marshall stated in his *Principles of Economics* that people will spend their money according to their values. When they place importance on saving and becoming wealthy, they'll save *first,* before paying the bills. If someone puts these priorities down at the bottom of the list, there will be "month left" at the end of the money, rather than money left at the end of the month. Everything will get in the way of setting funds aside, everyone else will get paid, and there goes all the cash.

Incidentally, this has nothing to do with how much you make; it has everything to do with your priorities. Your goals determine whether you'll be rich or poor, scraping along or spreading pâté on pricey little crackers. No doubt you've heard the stories of those people who make a modest salary, save religiously, and leave an estate worth in the millions. You've probably also heard about people who earn heaps of money but leave only a pile of debt to their heirs. It's all a question of what's most important to the one holding the purse strings.

Look at how you use money in your life. Do you squirrel it away? Are you an investor or a risk taker? Do you spend lots on clothes, education, or travel? Do you throw lavish parties, keep your cash to yourself, or donate to charities? Are you saving for specific items, such as children's education, retirement, or buying a prize-winning pig or a 50-foot yacht? Does most of your spending happen in the realm of business, home, or the community—or something else?

Simply put, where does it all go? As is often said, follow the money. It leaves a trail straight to your values.

5. Where Are You Most Organized?

Your hierarchy of values leaves additional clues in the areas where you're most organized.

- Your highest goal will be the most ordered part of your life (with little or no chaos).

- There's greater confusion in your less-important endeavors, so other people tend to control you in these areas.

- Your lowest-priority objectives will require outside motivation to get you to pay attention and complete them.

Again, we can consider the surgeon as an example. Everything relating to her medical career was in absolute order, from her thoughts about it to her reference library to her surgical equipment. If you'd looked at her kitchen (and she would have been chagrined to show it to you), you would have wondered how a woman of her professional precision and intimate understanding of germs could stand to use it. Bottom line? Her environment revealed where the true passion was held. **Order equals high value, and chaos equals low value—it's as simple as that.**

Ask yourself, *Where's the greatest order in my life? Where do things run most smoothly with the least amount of volatility? Where's the greatest chaos? Where do things seem unpredictable and erratic?*

6. Where Are You Most Disciplined?

Nobody has to get you up in the morning to do what's most important to you. You can easily focus on that which you truly care about. Whenever you unwisely label yourself as "flighty" or "undisciplined," it's because there's something else higher up in your value system vying for your attention, and you expect yourself to live otherwise. Whenever you think that you're flaky, you really aren't. You're just trying to live someone else's mission at that moment, someone you've given authority to. Everyone's focused somewhere—nothing's missing because you have every trait. So where are you consistently on task?

7. What Do You Think About?

Who hasn't had an unexpected idea in the shower or while driving? When you have time to think but your hands are occupied, your mind probably takes the opportunity to present you with whatever it's been working on—consciously or unconsciously—for days, weeks, or even years.

Your values tend to interrupt your "regularly scheduled programming." You'll be having lunch with a friend when your mind will begin to wander, and thoughts of something other than what's on the menu—both figuratively and literally—will pop up. You may find yourself thinking about work even when you're at home, or vice versa. If you're frequently distracted by ideas about one thing while you're involved with something else, what are those thoughts?

Then again, you may spend a good part of your day consciously choosing to think about certain things. Your vocation (or avocation) may cause you to focus on specific topics for hours at a time. **What are you constantly mulling over, considering, and trying to understand even more?**

The Bible declares: "For as he thinketh in his heart, so is he." Look to your thoughts and learn who you are.

8. What Do You Visualize?

One woman I know loves music. She doesn't have mundane imaginings of playing MP3 files on her computer, of course. Her dreams take her onto the stage, where she stars as Carmen, the great mezzo-soprano herself, draped in beautiful costumes, fluttering a delicate Spanish fan, and receiving the adulation of an enormous audience. In real life, my friend doesn't aspire to this, but she does hold season tickets to the Santa Fe Opera. She loves to dress up to go see the performances and gets a wonderful feeling from being in the audience when the curtain rises and the first notes emerge from the orchestra pit. She also imagines that someday she'll choose a world-class diva to follow around the globe for a season so that she can enjoy all the ups and downs of an entire tour, watching the singer perform all the great operatic roles.

These dreams, images, and real-life plans reveal this woman's love of performance—specifically classical musical theater. Her profession is graphic design, but music is high on her passions list. Not only does it provide the score for her daydreams, but it's evident in each of the other categories listed in this chapter:

- Her home showcases opera paraphernalia.

- She works for an advertising agency that creates marketing materials for the local opera.

- She's planning and talking with her friends about the next season even before this one has concluded, and so on.

There are commonalities in the landscape of your dreams, both waking and sleeping. **What do you imagine for yourself?** What's your vision for your life? When you daydream and imagine your future, what's the recurring theme?

9. What Do You Talk to Yourself About?

You, like everyone else, engage in self-talk, some of which builds you up and some of which tears you down. But all of it ultimately hones in on what's most important. You even have an internal dialogue where parts of you converse with each other. **What are those conversations about?**

You may debate actions you "should" take . . . which ones do you discuss with yourself? Perhaps you evaluate other people or opportunities or weigh your skills and talents, making lists of pros and cons about any variety of things. You may design plans for yourself or your family, your home or business ventures, or your next vacation. What's the subject of your inner dialogue?

You're constantly talking to yourself about what's really most important, what you'd love to manifest in your life. You're continually running affirmations or words of power through your mind, both constructive and destructive ones, and these color and even generate your perceptions in life. All of these internal dialogues revolve around your strongest desires.

10. What Do You Speak about with Others?

Most people have a way of bringing the conversation around to their favorite topics sooner or later. Have you ever noticed how these people who share the same interests waste no time in discovering this delightful coincidence? Or how someone will occasionally monopolize the discussion with the object of their fascination, ultimately to the bemusement and even boredom of the rest of the group?

When I was consulting with some doctors in Miami recently, one of them complained to me that a colleague was irritating because he was more interested in talking with me about my days as a surf bum than having me get busy coaching them. "I tell you what," the doctor said. "He'd rather go surfing than practice healing any day of the week."

It isn't hard to discern the second doctor's hierarchy of values, is it? Surfing comes before medicine; adventure (or perhaps freedom or self-expression) comes before career development. His irritated colleague, though, was all business:

Within five minutes he was on task and talking about the issues in his practice that he was hoping to resolve with my help. Professional achievement was clearly high on his ideals list.

When you meet someone new, what do you find yourself chatting about most? When you're with old friends, what topics do you revisit time and again? What conversations captivate you and keep you interested for the longest period of time?

11. What Do You React To?

What grabs your attention, either by pulling you in or repelling you? If I were to include something here that supports your values, you'd be apt to smile and be open to what you're reading, but if I mention an idea that challenges your interests, you may be put off and frown or even get bored.

How have you been reacting to each of the examples I've used so far? If you find yourself thinking, *Yes, that's right,* I'm probably using stories that resonate with your top values. If, on the other hand, you find yourself wondering, *Who on earth does that?* I've simply included illustrations that don't reflect your goals.

The same is true in your interactions with anyone you meet, anyplace you visit, and any event you experience. **Observe what you pay attention to. Notice what makes you smile and frown, and what makes you lean in to hear more or shut down, folding your arms in front of your body.** (Also recognize that, as you talk to others, their facial expressions and body language reveal their value systems, too.) Stay aware, and this kind of positive and negative feedback will serve you in getting to know yourself incredibly well.

12. What Are Your Goals?

If you're a person who writes down goals and works toward them, simply consult your current list of objectives. Do they revolve around business, family, or vacations? Do you see a pattern here, too?

It's a pretty direct correlation. People who have financial aspirations high on their list will have goals revolving around income, investing, retirement, and so on. People who value mental aptitude will strive in academics, intellectual achievement, skill acquisition, and the like. Vocational ambitions will evoke career-advancement and professional-acknowledgment goals; while physical targets will inspire focus on body fat, blood chemistry, and athletic accomplishment. Spiritual, familial, and social beliefs express themselves in typical fashion, especially for those who have these areas highest at the top of their list.

Pay attention to the act of making your list on a piece of paper. Wishes of higher importance are generally demonstrated by being written faster and more fluidly, having clearer details and broader content, being easier to read, and inspiring tears.

If you don't have written objectives, **simply consider what you'd most love to do, be, or have in your life, and which of those goals you're actively moving toward.** Which ones do you pursue nearly every day?

The Language of Values

You'll notice that I haven't put restrictions on the words to use in expressing your goals. Some people believe that values are more accurately understood as emotional ends—as states of feeling or being that you seek whenever you do or experience what's important to you. I tend to view them as multilayered. Expressing an ideal as *a beautiful home* may include desires of *self-expression, comfortable living space, and prestige,* or even *creating an environment where my spirit is nurtured and my body renewed.* Who can say which are the real values? Only the person expressing them knows. I suggest that you choose words that move you and speak to your heart. As you refine your values, take the opportunity to select more phrases that have deep meaning for you and tug at your soul.

Actions to Create More Fulfilling Relationships

— **Answer the 12 questions below.** If you observe and analyze yourself and your environment the way I've suggested, you'll discover what's truly important to you: Your life demonstrates it.

1. How do I fill my space? What themes do I see in the places where I spend most of my time?

2. How do I spend my time?

3. How do I spend my energy?

4. How do I spend my money? What do I invest in?

5. Where am I most organized? Where do I demonstrate the most order?

6. Where am I most disciplined? Where am I most reliable and focused?

7. What do I think about? What thoughts follow me wherever I go?

8. What do I visualize? What are my daydreams?

9. What do I speak to myself about? What is my internal dialogue?

10. What do I talk with others about? What is my external dialogue?

11. What do I react to? What makes me smile or frown?

12. What are my goals?

In your notebook, record the dominant three or four answers for each question. As you look at this information, notice the emerging patterns.

— **Rank your values.** Continue by using the following instructions for expressing and then ranking your priorities. I've included the most common terms for values and their definitions, yet you may find that you need to tweak the wording to make it just right for you. Forgo that process for right now, however, and concentrate on getting an order established.

1. Start by reading all 84 of the potential human-value terms/definitions that follow.

2. After you've read through them once, rank them within each category on a scale from 1 to 7, with 1 being the highest importance and 7 being the lowest. Record your ranking in the left column.

3. Filter your ranking through the answers to the 12 questions that you completed above. **The idea is to look at your values through the lens of what your life actually demonstrates.** Remember, you generally have space, time, energy, and money for what's truly important to you.

4. After you've given that due consideration, summarize—to the best of your ability—the top 12 values that your life demonstrates as being the most important to you. In other words, take the top 12 value terms/definitions (the ones that you gave a rating of "1" in the first series) and prioritize them into a second list, using the lines in the right-hand column. (Note that not every line in the second column will be filled in—only one line in each section will have a number on it.) Double-check their sequence by asking yourself, *When I have a decision to make between these goals, which does my life demonstrate that I keep choosing?* When your prioritized sequence matches what your life truly exhibits, you've found your current hierarchy of values.

5. Share what you've learned about yourself with a loved one, and invite him or her to provide feedback and then complete the process, too.

Value Terms/Definitions

Spiritual:

Connection: experiencing my soul or God ____ ____

Reflection: going inside myself; listening to my inner voice; seeing my inner vision ____ ____

Integrity: knowing and living my higher spiritual values ____ ____

Temperance: having a sense of balance and inner harmony within myself ____ ____

Discernment: seeing a higher order regardless of the apparent disorder of outer peace and war ____ ____

Inspiration: feeling a sense of purpose ____ ____

Identification: living from my divine vital core; being more spiritually than materially focused ____ ____

Authenticity: being genuine and truthfully honest with myself ____ ____

Surrender: modestly submitting or humbling myself to the grand divine design and order ____ ____

Unity: fitting into nature; feeling part of the whole ____ ____

Devotion: holding to religious faith and belief ____ ____

Personal responsibility: rising above judgment and beyond pardon or forgiveness ____ ____

Mental:

Wisdom: understanding the laws of the
universe—a mature understanding of my life ___ ___

Inquisitive curiosity: interested in everything;
exploring; loving to read and learn ___ ___

Intelligent thinking: reasoning and
analyzing logically ___ ___

Intuition: thinking/feeling spontaneously
and instinctively ___ ___

Discernment: making choices and decisions ___ ___

Associating or dissociating: attaching or
detaching freely ___ ___

Prioritizing and planning: self-discipline;
self-restraint; resistance to temptation ___ ___

Imagination: creative and unique thinking ___ ___

Development: increasing mental acuity ___ ___

Actualization: awakening the genius within ___ ___

Broad-minded: open to different ideas and
beliefs ___ ___

Adventure: seeking stimulating experiences;
having a mentally exciting life ___ ___

Vocational:

Inspiration: serving a higher purpose or calling ___ ___

Self-direction: choosing my own goals; doing what I love; actualizing my own career dreams ___ ___

Independence: self-reliant, self-sufficient ___ ___

Ambition: aspiring, working hard, and achieving goals ___ ___

Leadership: inspiring others to greater productivity ___ ___

Growth: attracting a greater quality and quantity of clients/customers/attendees/patients ___ ___

Quality: providing greater service to clients ___ ___

Excellence: mastering the skills of my profession; pursuing excellence; being number one ___ ___

Accountability: embracing consequences for decisions and actions ___ ___

Competence: being more capable, efficient, and effective in my business ___ ___

Professionalism: adhering to behavioral and appearance guidelines ___ ___

Responsible: obedient; dutiful; meeting obligations; being dependable and reliable ___ ___

Financial:

Perspective: appreciating the importance of
money and valuing what it offers humanity ___ ___

Ingenuity: searching for creative ways and
means to serve and make money ___ ___

Prudence: making deals; creative financial
negotiations; shopping for bargains ___ ___

Balance: maintaining fair exchange,
reciprocity, and non-indebtedness ___ ___

Security: saving money; investing ___ ___

Development: building self-worth and
self-respect ___ ___

Savvy: balancing emotions to more effectively
and consistently manage money ___ ___

Acumen: managing; budgeting; or spending
money, energy, and resources wisely ___ ___

Growth: building wealth/net worth; amassing
a fortune and material possessions ___ ___

Taking chances: calculating and taking
risks; speculating ___ ___

Protection: preserving wealth ___ ___

Contribution: philanthropy and charity ___ ___

Familial:

Attention: spending time connecting or
interacting with family members   ____ ____

Fulfillment: setting realistic expectations with
relationships; breaking fantasies and myths   ____ ____

Clear communication: dissolving judgments
and communicating in terms of values   ____ ____

Intimacy: sharing love and sex in a
mature fashion   ____ ____

Resolution: managing conflict with family
of origin or family of choice   ____ ____

Caring: meeting the needs of others   ____ ____

Providing: creating a quality home for
family members   ____ ____

Security: safety for loved ones   ____ ____

Respect: honoring parents, elders, and others ____ ____

Inspiring: encouraging children to achieve
their own path of full potential   ____ ____

Educating: helping children expand
their opportunities   ____ ____

Adventure: traveling on vacations
and exploring with loved ones   ____ ____

Social:

Leadership: leading or commanding
others for a worthy cause   ____ ____

Power: desiring prominence, authority,
control, or influence over others and events   ____ ____

Recognition: respect; approval from others;
maintaining public image   ____ ____

Order: initiating transformation; raising
socioeconomic standards and stability   ____ ____

Contribution: working for the welfare
of humankind   ____ ____

Equality: equal opportunity for all   ____ ____

Belonging: feeling that others care
about me   ____ ____

Security: protection from self or an enemy ____ ____

Justice: upholding ethical and legal
principles; righting perceived wrongs   ____ ____

Respect: honoring rights to dignity; independence or privacy; good manners; courtesy   ____ ____

Friendship: shared loyalty to, and empathy
for, friends or group   ____ ____

Tradition: preservation of time-honored customs ____ ____

Physical:

Well-being: maximum health ____ ____

Nutrition: maximizing or maintaining good eating habits ____ ____

Moderation: integrating extremes of sensation or action ____ ____

Building strength and tone: exercising and stretching muscles ____ ____

Vitality: increasing endurance and stamina; keeping active ____ ____

Maintaining beauty/handsomeness: clean, neat, well presented or dressed, and tidy ____ ____

Self-indulgent gratification of physical desires: enjoying food, sex, leisure, etc. ____ ____

Seeking daring adventures: taking risks ____ ____

Aesthetics: appreciating the beauty of nature and the arts ____ ____

Ecology: protecting the environment; preserving nature ____ ____

Independence: spontaneous action; freedom to travel the world ____ ____

Variety: a life filled with challenge, novelty, and change ____ ____

Allow yourself the time to record what you observe, pause and reflect, and then complete the ranking. Your list is an ongoing process, not a static thing. It's an incredible tool for self-awareness, and you'll require this clarity as you move on to the next chapter, which will help you link your values to those of your loved ones.

Words of Power

I know myself.

I pay close attention to what my life demonstrates as truly important.

I live by my values and I am fulfilled.

I expect myself to act only according to what means the most to me.

I expect others to stay true to their beliefs.

I am grateful for what is, as it is.

❋❋❋ ❋❋❋

CHAPTER FOUR

Linking What You Love with What They Love

If you want to move people, it has to be toward a vision that's positive
for them, that taps important values, that
gets them something they desire . . .
— Martin Luther King, Jr.

Certain individuals just seem to know how to speak straight from the heart and directly to the souls of others, to communicate with their inner spirits. They're able to move people to work together; respect one another; and take powerful, collaborative action. Some of these insightful, inspiring men and women become leaders of significant societal movements or of major companies, while others have less public influence and do their magic in the realms of community, family, friendships, and romantic partnerships.

In some circles, people think we need to regroup and return to a shared morals system, and supposedly that will make all of society's woes go away. Equally baffling, some relationship counselors tell singles to seek mates with values similar to their own; and that will be the key to long-lasting love . . . but they're not telling the whole story.

It's true that people need to find connections on this level if they hope to move forward together. Here's the twist, though: It's not necessary for people to cherish the same things. What's far more important is that the values are simply *linked*. Then everyone can feel that their inner truths are being served by the activities of everyone involved, whether they're a couple, a company, or an activist organization.

In this chapter, you'll learn more about what it means to link your values with another person, see how you can do so even when it appears impossible, and get clear on what happens if you overlook something this important.

We All Want to Be Loved for Who We Really Are

Martha and Tom each revere certain things in life, and both have a sense that their highest beliefs (what's most important to them) somehow reveal who they really are. These values help shape their identities in the world and reflect their most personal sense of self. They do everything they can to live according to these principles, and it's important to them that they also feel respected or even honored for this, rather than simply thwarted in their efforts.

So far, this couple isn't unique. In fact, they're just like you, me, and everyone else. Don't you want to be loved for being yourself, not for trying to be what someone else imagines you "ought" to be?

Several years ago, Martha worked in marketing and was known among her peers as a talented direct mail specialist. When she and her husband decided to start their family, she chose to put her career on hold and focus her attention on their children. It was more important to her to be the primary caregiver so that she could be with their kids during key developmental years than it was for her to pursue her profession. Keep in mind that this was a decision based on her values—neither right nor wrong in the abstract, but absolutely in line with what was most important to *her*.

Tom agreed with this. It was crucial to him that his kids be given the kind of childhood that he felt he'd never had, where at least one parent could be available pretty much all the time. He knew he wasn't cut out for that role because too much of his sense of self-worth and contribution, both to the family and to the wider world, was tied to his work life. He loved the fact that Martha was not only willing, but eager, to take on that responsibility, and his income would allow them to do this together.

For many years, it worked out as planned. Martha felt fulfilled in her day-to-day life, focusing on the family. She was grateful for her husband's contribution and appreciated it immensely that his salary was allowing her to dedicate herself to their home life. Tom was content in their arrangement, too. He was frequently overcome with emotion when they spent time together because he realized that he was able to provide for a life where his children could grow up in the loving care of his wife. And he was able to do this because he excelled in his job, doing work that he loved—work he had loved, that is, until recently.

These days, Tom and Martha are upset with one another and aren't seeing eye to eye. Tom's had some setbacks in his profession and now he'd like to make a change, but Martha fears that her husband's quest to "find himself" will leave their family financially vulnerable. When he complains that she just doesn't understand what it's like for him, she offers to go back to work (not sincerely, but more as a dig at his ability to provide for the family). He jabs back by insisting that whatever child care they might be able to secure will cost far more than what she can earn, given that she's been out of the job market for many years. Besides, does she really want to put her little ones in the hands of some stranger? (That's his one-two punch at her professional worth and her maternal responsibility.)

She fires back, "What are we supposed to do, just start eating cereal for dinner and put the kids' college-savings plans on hold? I'm not sacrificing our children's future just because you're having a midlife crisis!" (Unspoken fantasy: *He should be more concerned about the family than his own selfish desires. He should just buckle down and make sure we're secure. This is the deal we made: I take care of the family at home, and he works and provides for us financially.*)

He replies, "What do you expect from me? Should I stay with this job I hate because you've become accustomed to a lavish lifestyle? I feel trapped by this huge house, the car, the private schools—all of it!" (Unspoken fantasy: *She should get off my back. Can't she see how hard I work? All she does is spend every penny I make. If she were more careful with our money, I wouldn't have to stay in this rat race just to make ends meet.*)

In this not-so-uncommon scenario, Martha's sense of security for herself and her family is being threatened, and Tom feels as if he's losing his personal autonomy. They're no longer connected through the values that may have bound them together at other times. The links have been cut for the moment, at least. This kind of detachment can affect the whole relationship, unless Martha and Tom reestablish some of their bonds.

They're angry, and barriers have gone up between them. Previously, he'd called whatever she'd done to support his mission "good." Now that his beliefs are challenged, he labels those same actions "bad." The same is true for Martha: She'd identified his behaviors as "good" whenever they'd supported her objectives, and now they're "bad" because she thinks they don't.

Incidentally, that's what we mean when we talk about ethics and morals. Whatever we do that supports or challenges our own inner truths gets deemed good or bad (morals), and we use a related set of "rules" to judge other people's behavior (ethics).

If we were able to wave a wand and cause Tom and Martha to start thinking more about what the other person values and working to connect the dots, they'd instantly change how they feel. They'd also ease up on their "rules" about what they have to do and be in order to get so-called love from one another. The more two people believe they're in alignment, the greater the freedom they give one another. It's easy to see how a change in perspective and objective would impact the conversation in this situation. These two could move from "what I fear" (opposed or unlinked) to "what we both would love" (aligned, or at least linked), and from "protect my value" (opposed or unlinked) to "honor one another's values" (aligned or linked).

Martha might say, "Tom, I'd love for you to feel fulfilled in your professional work because I care about you. I can see that you're dissatisfied, and I know you want to have a career that has greater challenges and rewards. Plus, I think it's important for us to show the kids that it's possible to do what you love and make a wonderful income. My fear is that we don't have the financial bridge we'll need while you're in transition. I realize that some of our expenses may be contributing to the pressure you're feeling, so let's put our heads together to see how we can best manage the money with as little impact on the family as possible."

Tom might reply, "Yes, I understand why that's important, and I don't want to jeopardize you or the children while I'm in this 'seeking' mode. Let's work on a transition plan; in fact, I'd love to build in some things we can do together as a family that will teach the kids about balancing responsibility with following your heart. We can use this as an opportunity to share important strategies for money management and budgeting, too. They're old enough now, and we can make it fun and rewarding for them while I decide on my next steps professionally."

How a Relationship Becomes Vulnerable

If Tom and Martha make this switch, they can begin to rebuild and navigate this potentially tricky transition with grace. If they don't ever get to this place of seeing how their values can be intertwined, both of them will continue to fantasize that if the other were different (aka "more like me"), life would be better. In fact, the relationship will become vulnerable if they continue living under this myth and dishonoring one another by resisting what's most important to each of them, which develops distance and opposition. Their bond will become equally weakened if someone gives in and allows one person's values to eclipse the other's. That creates the need for distance, which nature will eventually provide—one way or another.

Imagine that Martha, still steaming from her latest exchange with her husband, goes to the gym to burn off her anger. While she's huffing and puffing on the elliptical machine, a guy working out next to her delivers this unoriginal opening line: "You know, you have such beautiful eyes! Are you a model?"

If her values were being fulfilled at home, she'd probably just say thank you, put on headphones, and turn up the volume on her music. Since she's feeling a lack of support (due to her perceptions), she may be willing to strike up a conversation with him.

If he starts talking with her about what's meaningful to her, beware. Suppose he says, "What's important to you? Oh, you have kids? I love kids! I have two of my own. What are your hopes for them? What are your dreams for you? What do you want most out of life . . . ?"

If this new guy pays attention to her desires and communicates directly to them, you can guess what might happen. *People will only behave in accordance with their own beliefs.* If she doesn't perceive her values as being honored and met at home, she'll naturally gravitate to a new situation. This is one of the primary reasons for infidelity, which will be discussed in greater detail in a later chapter.

Now, suppose Tom finds out what's going on. His wife is having intimate, values-fulfilling conversations with another man—and maybe engaging in other highly satisfying activities, too. Tom can get angry and blow up at Martha, which would be a poor strategy if he wants to sustain his relationship with her. Flying off the handle would put up another barrier. It would reinforce her perception of him as an obstruction, blocking her from realizing her desires, even with someone else.

The wise man will take a few steps back. He'll find out what's really going on—what this guy is doing for and with his wife that he hasn't been, attempting to learn from someone who's doing something "right" in her eyes. He'll take some time to discover her true priorities—how she spends her time, energy, and money; what she talks and thinks about; and so on. Then he'll start communicating with her more *in terms of her values.*

My objective in laying this out for you is not to justify infidelity; instead, it's to point out the significance of values in the longevity and sustained exclusivity of a relationship. If those things are important to you, then you're wise to attend to this. If you believe that your ideals aren't being respected in a relationship, know that you're vulnerable to temptation. And if you aren't paying attention to your mate's highest goals, then you're helping set him or her up for an unfulfilling relationship or potential affair.

This is true in commerce, too: Connections with your customers, employees, co-workers, or vendors all can become vulnerable if you don't attend to their values. You're kidding yourself if you think that their loyalty to you will win out; the minute the relationship stops satisfying their needs, they'll hit the road—or attempt to undermine or otherwise try to put distance between you in some other way. Remember this: *People are only faithful to their own value system.*

Let's take this a step further. Don't expect loyalty from someone because it doesn't come from another person. The same holds true for commitment and trustworthiness. This may be shocking, but let it sink in for a minute: All of these qualities come from you, in relationship to another. If you've looked at how people spend their time, money, energy, conversations, and thinking, only then have you identified their core truths—not what they say or what they're infatuated with, and certainly not what you project onto them, but their inner values as demonstrated by their lives. If you can communicate your values in terms of theirs more effectively than anyone else on the planet, then you can create what some would call a real, loyal, trusting, and committed relationship. (By my definition, though, commitment may not be what you're seeking. In my admittedly quirky worldview, being *committed* is when you've reached your limit and finally taken your loved one to the psychiatric hospital!)

Love for Sale?

If you'd love a long-term relationship with someone, then who's accountable for that? You are and no one else. Remember what you read about the caring, careful, and careless relationships in an earlier chapter? **The caring relationship is one where each person seeks to understand and honor the other just as he or she is, equally embracing both positives and negatives.** This reconnects you when you become distant (which is inevitable but not necessarily permanent) and gives you ever-increasing levels of intimacy, stability, and fulfillment. You can apply this in all situations, from romance to parenting to business.

Not only can you take a few lessons from personal connections and apply them to your professional life, but it works the other way, too. Communicating using someone's key concerns can be likened to the best sales processes. Consider the commonsense sequence of selling, which follows the same pattern as being caring (honoring someone's values) in an intimate relationship:

1. Greet and introduce yourself.

2. Gain rapport with the other person.

3. Establish a need, dominant buying motive, or highest value.

4. Confirm this information.

5. Offer a solution.

6. Close and confirm your data again.

7. Serve the person.

8. Get referrals.

Those are the steps to effective selling, and *they're exactly the same as the keys to a fulfilling relationship.*

Suppose I'm a single person at a party or club, and one of my desires at that moment is to have sex with someone. My probability for fulfilling that wish is low if I walk up to a woman and ask, "Would you like to have sex with me?"

Instead, what if I walk up and say, "Hi, I'm John Demartini. Who are you?" I greet and introduce myself (Step 1).

After I get her name, I continue: "Where are you from?"

"San Diego," she responds, perhaps guardedly.

"Oh, I've been there often. Do you know where the downtown Omni is? I've been going there for ten years. Where do you live in San Diego?"

"Just a few streets over, on Columbia."

"Wow, I bet I go right by there when I'm in town, because I like to jog around the hotel. What a coincidence!" I've now started the conversation and am finding things that we have in common. Gaining rapport (Step 2) is simply asking questions and behaving in ways that reveal similarity and commonality. Once I've gained this connection, I can start asking more personal questions.

"What's it like to live in San Diego? Do you have to deal with traffic much? Are there specific shops you like?" At this point, I'm trying to establish needs (Step 3), looking for the frustrations and voids in her life. I can never offer her a solution if I haven't established a need or a problem, so I must look until I find one. Then, when I discover something, I confirm it (Step 4), rather than just assuming that I understand:

"Okay, let me get this straight: You say that San Diego is kind of a sports town, but you enjoy cultural activities more, the traffic is a pain in the neck, you really miss the rolling hills of North Carolina, and you're looking to move back East?"

"Yes, that's right."

"You know, I have a friend who's running a wonderful bed-and-breakfast in downtown Baltimore. The city is really fun because there's plenty to do right there, but it doesn't take long before you're out in the country with those rolling hills. Would you like her number? She'd be a terrific contact if you thought you'd like to explore that area. Plus, I travel all over the world, so if there's ever a place you'd like to go and you need to connect with someone there, let me know. I can introduce you to great people just about anywhere. Do you think that might help?" I've now offered a solution (Step 5). Notice that everything is done by questions, never by telling someone what they need.

Also observe that I've already started linking what she'd like (a new hometown that meets some specific criteria) with what I love (travel) so that we can start to form a relationship of equals without minimization or maximization. The rest of my "sales process"—closing and serving—doesn't really require description, does it? (I left out Step 8, getting referrals, which would be new social contacts with friends, because it probably isn't as applicable to hooking up.) My objective may still be to have sex with this woman, but I'll do so through relationship building, linking what we love until she sees why having sex with me will be something that she'll enjoy, too.

Can you see how sales and personal relationship building are really incredibly similar? In both situations, you're wise to find out which of someone's values could be satisfied by the same actions (whatever those might be) that fulfill your own.

Link Your Love

If you can't see how someone else getting what they'd love gives you what you desire, then you'll naturally try to change him or her to your way, or you'll be compelled to find someone new. You can try to convince yourself to live and let live, but until you can see how to *love and link love,* you'll be drawn to something different.

You can learn how to do this with *anyone*—and that's not an exaggeration. You can, indeed, choose to link your values with anyone else's. Doing this is an art encompassing both proficiency and creativity, which can be learned and developed. It's the most important skill you'll probably ever apply in building, maintaining, and enriching personal ties. You can start today with your existing relationships by listing the top five values for you and for the other person, then creating a web of connections. (You'll get more detailed instructions at the end of this chapter.)

The more intertwined you make these webs, the easier it is to talk with others, to work out perceived differences and problems, and to enrich your relationships with an even deeper sense of intimacy and connectedness.

Furthermore, I suggest that you reduce insignificant conversations. Because you build fellowship through meaning-filled communication, if you feel that you simply can't see your way to making a subject important to you, or if you prefer not to make the effort to do so, you'd be wise to move on. One-sided conversations, or alternating monologues, are characterized by one person speaking about what's meaningful to him or her, and the other's mind wandering away to his or her own concerns. Either link your values, shift the conversation, or move on, because monologues are almost a sure setup for disappointing or dissatisfying relationships.

I'm certain, as you'll discover for yourself as you read on, that you can make whatever is essential to others equally valuable to you if you choose to and apply the methods in this book. Then you can engage in a true dialogue, where you both care enough about one another's values that you love to listen because it helps you do and be what you love . . . and you enjoy talking about whatever leads you both to your dreams.

The master of relationships is the person who knows and applies the art of linking someone else's values to his or her own and can communicate with anyone's ideals.

Do Values Change?

Certainly, major milestones can cause priorities to shift. A life-threatening illness, a midlife crisis, or the birth of a child—anything that triggers people to reassess and rethink what's important to them—may alter a belief system, either reordering things or introducing new values altogether. That's why it's crucial to continue to talk about your values with those whom you care about: Everyone needs to stay attuned to what may have changed.

You can consciously choose to make a shift, by the way. You can intentionally give yourself a "midlife crisis," rather than wait for whatever life seems to hand you. You might decide to do this if you're ready for different results in your life.

Let's say you've been single for a long time. Because you've gone through the process of figuring out your highest concerns, plus you've gotten feedback from former romantic interests, you're aware that familial and social values rank dead last for you—and you realize that may not be ideal if you want to create a so-called committed relationship with someone. Or perhaps you want to make a change in the course of your financial life: You'd like to start amassing some wealth, but you know it won't happen until you raise your ranking of saving and investing.

Here's how to do it: Write 100 to 200 benefits of how the value that you'd love to elevate in your hierarchy can serve you. For the examples I just mentioned, what are 100 to 200 ways you'll be served by sharing your life with someone in a "committed" relationship? Or how will saving and investing benefit you?

Next, decide where you'd like this value to rank in your list. Take a look at the ones ranked higher and the one ranked lower, and write 100 to 200 specific benefits of how this new value will help you with each of the other two. Let's say you want to put the goal of saving money and building wealth between raising your children and traveling the world.

You'd ask yourself, *How will saving money and building wealth help me raise my children? How will saving money and building wealth help me travel the world?*

What you're doing is dissolving the perceived voids that determine your inner truths. In physics, a void is a separation in space-time, and so it is in your life. A value is that which you'd love to realize or fulfill at even greater levels—but right now you experience it as separation. When you shift your priorities, you change your perception of what's lacking (higher priority voids/values) and what's abundant (fulfilled, and therefore lower priority, voids/values). You actually comprehend a greater oneness with things that are lower on your ranking system because they appear already more fulfilled or satisfied and, therefore, less important to strive for. They seem sufficient or adequate at that moment.

I guarantee that this exercise works. It causes your brain to rewire itself and see new possibilities that it didn't before. It gives you more reasons—ones that you already thought were important—to attend to the newly elevated goal. This is similar to the linking exercise you'll be doing to connect your own and someone else's values; it's just that you're speaking to yourself in terms of your own beliefs.

You can actually change your destiny by altering your hierarchy of values. In other words, your priorities dictate your destiny because they move you toward or away from certain things in life. Remember that if you decide to align your values to support you in achieving specific goals, you're wise to choose those that are reasonable and truly attainable. A wish for only a "happy" marriage forever and ever isn't reasonable, but a goal of being with someone who contributes to balancing you by both supporting and challenging you so that you can experience what's most inspiring to your heart—now that's reasonable *and* attainable. This includes the understanding that someone will equilibrate you, bringing you down when you're inflated or experiencing an extreme high, and vice versa, so that together you can participate in the journey of learning about each other and yourselves.

Another Way to Think about Linking

Let's picture two individuals as spheres, three-dimensional circles. If two people haven't yet discovered, or think they can't find, anything in common, they're alienated, resentful, and opposed. The spheres are completely separate.

Figure 1. **Resentment:** Two spheres are separated and in opposition.

If two people are infatuated with one another, seeing everything the same and perceiving no differences, the spheres are right on top of one another with little or no distinction between them. The two individuals seem to fuse into one, as one person minimizes him- or herself and figuratively disappears.

Figure 2. **Infatuation:** One of the two spheres seems to disappear, as it's eclipsed by the other.

The most stable position can be pictured as the joining of two spheres where the overlap is equal. The resulting third form, found in the middle, is called a *vesica pisces.*

Figure 3. **Unity Within Duality:** The two spheres remain separate but connected. (The *vesica pisces* is the third shape created by the joining of the two.)

The *vesica pisces* (Latin for "vessel of the fish") has a fascinating history. The shape has had sacred significance for as far back as symbolism of any kind has been around. In ancient religions, the sphere represented the supreme being, without beginning or end and flawlessly symmetrical. Add a second sphere, and together they symbolize the two facets of creation, god and goddess. In the *vesica pisces,* divine connection, the unity within the duality, was revealed.

In ancient pagan traditions, this shape came to signify various individual goddesses (most notably Venus), as well as the female genitalia, the sacred portal through which divinity emanates into the material world. Likewise, in medieval art, the Christ child and the Virgin Mary were often depicted inside this shape, called a *mandorla* (Italian for "almond") in this context. You can also see it in Gothic cathedral architecture, usually in archways, symbolizing the doorway between the material and spiritual realms. Early Christians adopted the motif in the form of the icthus, or "Jesus fish," signifying Jesus of Nazareth as the *vesica pisces* himself—the go-between for God and humankind, for heaven and earth. Still other adaptations and interpretations abound.

Let's add the idea of a relationship between two people characterized by a sacred unity within the duality of coupledom. This means that you don't have totally independent lives, nor are you too dependent on each other. You're both free and constrained; you have mutually interdependent lives. You each have your own purpose and objective, and you also have overlapping goals.

To recap:

- With separate spheres, you have two unrelated purposes.

- In an overwhelming infatuation, you have what you think is one purpose, but one of you loses your individuality.

- When you and another have your own purposes, plus an overlapping one, you have a doorway from the material world of mundane concerns to the spiritual realm, where all is love and creativity abounds.

Wisdom is honoring other people's value systems, knowing they're going to live by them no matter what, and learning to truly love and appreciate that. Continually ask yourself, *How are my highest values served by them doing what they love?* You'll find again and again that whatever you're challenged to embrace in a person represents your own disowned part—the one that ranks low on your list.

The purpose of relationships is to attract into your life what you disown in yourself, to bring that which is lower in your belief hierarchy into your field of attention so that you can learn to love that part of yourself and recognize your wholeness. That is your *vesica pisces:* You can find the divine unity within perceived duality, as the sacred perfection of the universe endlessly unfolds.

Actions to Create More Fulfilling Relationships

— **Link your values.** List your top five values on one side of a piece of paper, and write someone else's top five on the other side; ideally, you'll choose someone who is significant to you, such as your mate or partner—someone you'd love to communicate with more effectively and appreciate more. (Return to the earlier chapters if you need help identifying your values.)

Now think of at least five ways in which the other person's top value helps you fulfill your first priority. Next, list at least five ways in which your top value helps the other person fulfill theirs.

Then go down the list: Write down five ways in which each of the other person's values supports your highest priority and each item on your list contributes to their number one value. Continue this process for the four remaining items for each person, giving ways in which each one of your values is beneficial for every one of the other person's, and vice versa. When this is done, a new door for communication and (if desired) intimacy is opened.

Here's a short example of what linking only the first and first, first and second, and second and second values might look like:

My #1 Value: FAMILY	My Mate's #1 Value: FINANCIAL SUCCESS
How my mate's #1 value of *financial success* helps me fulfill my value of *family:*	How my #1 value of *family* helps my mate fulfill his value of *financial success:*

My #1 Value: FAMILY / My Mate's #1 Value: FINANCIAL SUCCESS

How my mate's #1 value of *financial success* helps me fulfill my value of *family:*

- Frees me to choose the kind of child care we want and if we want it at all.
- Presents the kids with a role model for making plenty of money while doing what you love.
- Enables us to have the resources to plan for our children's future and even see beyond that to our grandchildren and other descendants.
- Provides amazing opportunities to travel as a family and experience wonderful vacations together.
- Gives all of us a sense of security and comfort that allows us to focus on other endeavors.

How my #1 value of *family* helps my mate fulfill his value of *financial success:*

- Keeps him aware that there's more to life than work, so he's more "human" and likable in the business world.
- Creates a beautiful home environment that's warm and inviting for entertaining colleagues and clients, and for deal making.
- Constantly teaches him the crucial moneymaking skills of true listening and staying in the present moment.
- Ensures that there's always nutritious food in the house so that he doesn't have to think about eating right and keeping his energy up.
- Forces him to take a rest every now and then so that he can go back to work revitalized.

My #2 Value: SPIRITUAL CONNECTION / My Mate's #2 Value: PROFESSIONAL DEVELOPMENT

How my mate's #1 value of *financial success* helps me fulfill my value of *spiritual connection:*

- Gives me the resources to dedicate parts of our home as "retreat" spaces.
- Helps me see how monetary pursuits can be infused with spiritual intention.
- Allows me to give generously to organizations and places of worship in which I believe.
- Enables me to perceive the similarities between financial prowess and spiritual guidance.
- Grants me the freedom to focus on elevated ideas instead of our survival.

How my #1 value of *family* helps my mate fulfill his value of *professional development:*

- Gives him common ground to discuss with his peers.
- Provides him with various mentors from my side of the family.
- Opens doors to professional opportunities through my connections with the kids' schools and extracurricular activities.
- Inspires him to continue to love learning the way the children do.
- Nurtures him so that he feels ready to take risks at work.

My #2 Value (Continued)	My Mate's #2 Value (Continued)
How my mate's #2 value of *professional development* helps me fulfill my value of *spiritual connection:* • Grounds me in practical action so that I don't become a spiritual "space cadet." • Introduces me to people with all kinds of beliefs, which reinforces or expands my own beliefs. • Gives me opportunities to find the holy in the seemingly mundane. • Provides me with time alone to pursue my spiritual practice. • Takes me to parts of the world I might not otherwise seek or see.	How my #2 value of *spiritual connection* helps my mate fulfill his value of *professional development:* • Keeps his mind open about what will "work" and what won't. • Challenges his intellect and reminds him to approach new things with a student's mind and heart. • Helps him appreciate where he is right now while he strives for the next level—teaches him to love himself and others whether they're "achieving" or not. • Creates an environment that spurs learning and inspiration. • Gives him "permission" to pursue what he loves.

Continue doing this until you've found at least 250 ways in which each of you doing and being what you love helps the other pursue his or her dreams.

250 Links

Your Top Five Values   Their Top Five Values

_____   _____

_____   _____

_____   _____

_____   _____

_____   _____

Imagine the many new connections you can discover through this method. It works wonders if you pursue it. If you can't see the union between what's important to another person and yourself, you have little or no reason to be in a relationship. The more links you make and the stronger the bonds, the more you'll have to communicate about, and the easier it is to understand each other. Instead of living with alternating monologues, you'll begin to experience meaningful dialogues. This is essential to any lasting partnership.

This exercise of identifying your values and someone else's, and then linking them to the best of your ability, is an ongoing process. You'll be doing it for the rest of your life, and the wonderful result is that you'll not only communicate more effectively and enrich the relationship, but you'll also become more grateful for one another.

— **Reevaluate on a regular basis.** For key relationships, I recommend that you discern your values, and the other person's, on a quarterly basis. Every three months, stop and look at what's important to each of you in life right now. If you don't know, observe and ask! I advise you to schedule this quarterly linking because it saves you valuable time in the long run. Aren't your relationships worth it?

Words of Power

I link what I love with what others care about.

I take the time to find out what other people value.

I find the divine unity within perceived duality.

I am grateful for the differences in people's value systems. I can see the sacred perfection.

I make and take time to communicate with those I love.

※※※ ※※※

CHAPTER FIVE

The Demartini Method for Neutralizing Emotions

The world of ideas which it discloses or illuminates,
the contemplation of divine beauty and order which it induces,
the harmonious connexion of its parts, the infinite hierarchy and
absolute evidence of the truths with which it is concerned, these, and
such like, are the surest grounds . . . were the plan of the universe
unrolled like a map at our feet, and the mind of man qualified to
take in the whole scheme of creation at a glance.
— J. J. Sylvester

Throughout this book, you've read repeatedly that whatever other people do that gets under your skin represents traits you simply haven't yet learned to love in yourself. You may have wondered, *Okay, then, how am I supposed to figure that out?* It's a reasonable question, and this chapter is all about helping you gain this wisdom for yourself through an experiential and intellectual process that I call The Demartini Method. You'll see it in action in the following example.

A woman in her 30s was dating an older man who was quite wealthy. He was just finishing up the legal proceedings of a divorce and was in no hurry to remarry, but she was feeling desperate and pressuring him to make a commitment. She badgered him constantly, and he kept telling her to back off.

They attended one of my programs because she was living with the hope that a self-improvement seminar would get them married—and he was hoping that it would convince her to ease up. (One of people's favorite illusions, at least in the world where I live every day, is that persuading others to attend a personal-development program will make them convert their values. Often, someone will call me with this request: "Please fix my partner!")

To the man's delight, I confronted the woman about her desperation. Feeling that she had to have him in a hurry, I explained, was a sign that she was minimizing herself and exaggerating him. She thought he was a "great catch" and that she ought to reel him in right away. In addition, she was attempting to impose marriage on him, thereby trying to eclipse his values. It was a perceptually unbalanced relationship.

I asked her, "So what's in it for him? When you get married, what do you have to offer? Do you have some kind of special spiritual awareness?"

"Well, no," she said, "not really."

"Are you some mental genius with incredible intellect?"

"No, I can't say that."

"Do you have a major business that provides jobs for thousands of people?"

"No, I'm not working for myself."

"Do you have great financial power—a trust fund, an inheritance, or a divorce settlement, something like that?"

"No, I'm in debt."

"Well, do you have a wonderful familial background? Are you especially adept at nurturing a family and marriage?"

"I was married once before. I don't know my dad, and my mom and I don't talk."

"How about social contacts? Do you have a big network

that's going to be helpful to this relationship?"

"No, I come from a small town and keep to myself."

"What about physical health, beauty, and hot sex? Are you someone who's sexually fulfilling? Does he feel that he just can't get enough of you?"

She looked over at her man, and he sort of shrugged. "Well, we do okay there," she confessed. "I suppose there's better."

I inquired again, "So what's in it for him?"

She was flat, humbled. But it wasn't my aim to make her feel inadequate. My intention was to point out that all of these minimizations were merely thoughts she had about herself, her self-image. So I asked her, "Can you see that all these answers are based on your perceptions? I just asked you questions, and you responded that you're somewhat deficient in all these areas. That's why you're holding on to this guy: You think that you have little to offer. You believe that he has all those powers and you have less or none."

It was the common dynamic of the "underdog" seeking marriage, while the "overdog" preferred to hang on to perceived freedom. Put another way, when people are fractionated and disempowered (underdogs), they tend to have many personas and masks—they're in a state of "many-ness," which makes "the one" attractive. When they're integrated, listening to the soul, and thus empowered (overdogs), their facades fall away; they're in a state of oneness, which makes "many" attractive. This is an expression of the law of "the one and the many": When you have the many you look for the one, and vice versa.

When underdogs seek to get overdogs to commit to an exclusive relationship, it's an attempt to hang on to the more expansive, empowered person. That's why we have all these apt phrases: "tie down," "ball and chain," "great catch," and so on. They convey that visceral sense of what one believes is a greater power being roped to a lesser power. That's exactly what was happening with the couple at my seminar.

The woman realized that she was addicted to the man's power and felt that she had to have it, ultimately deceiving herself by believing she had none of her own. She feared that if she waited too long to get married, he'd find out who she really was, which in her mind was someone with little to offer.

We played with this concept—it wasn't about who she *actually* was, but about who she *thought* she was. I asked her, "Where do you have spiritual power and awareness?"

At first, it was difficult for her to answer, because she spent so much time in the illusion that she had none. As we pursued it—and I kept inquiring until she came up with a response—she awakened a vision of herself that expanded her self-awareness.

The condition of our lives is partly based upon the depth of the queries we or others bring up. When I asked her a few challenging questions, she unearthed some strong inner qualities that were already truly present but unseen. She *had* spiritual power and awareness, just in unique forms that were unappreciated.

Then we continued, looking for her mental genius—expressed according to her values, not his. I assured her, *"Nothing's missing.* It may be in a different area of life than someone else's, but you always have it. Where is it? Keep searching and you'll find it."

We spent the next three hours helping her realize where she had power in all seven areas. This is what you'll be doing with The Demartini Method in the next chapter: You'll list each trait that you strongly like and dislike in another person—both perceived positives and negatives—then you'll neutralize your emotional reaction to them by seeing how you have the exact same traits in equal proportion. Yes, *equal proportion.*

For every area of life in which you don't feel empowered, you'll usually connect with someone who appears strong in that aspect. As we identified this woman's strengths, her image of herself and of her worth escalated remarkably. We then also used The Demartini Method with her father as the subject, since it was clear that this relationship was driving her to believe that she must have a powerful, wealthy man in her life to fill in her perceived gaps. Her dad left when she was a child, and I helped her realize where the new forms of "father" had manifested, enabling her to stop seeing herself as someone who was missing a parent.

She understood that she'd developed a fantasy based on her religious upbringing: As long as she could get a man to marry her, he couldn't leave her as her father had. Yet in her first marriage, her husband had left, busting her illusion and leaving her feeling devastated and desperate. Then we had another subject for The Demartini Method: the first husband.

When she completed all of this self-examination, she was no longer frantic to land her guy *because she realized that she was his equal,* although she expressed it in her unique, value-driven forms. The moment she felt this, she knew that she didn't need to rush into marriage. Furthermore, she might explore her options and see which other men would appreciate her and her new vision of power in the world.

Interestingly enough, the moment she neutralized her attachment to the man at the program, he started to find her incredibly attractive. Remember the maxim: *Flee, they follow!*

Follow, they flee! This couple illustrated it right before our eyes. As she withdrew her infatuation and attempts to impose her values upon him and woke up to her own inner strength, he found her more desirable than ever.

We broke for lunch, and the two left together. When I returned to the room for the afternoon session, they were beaming and showing the other participants the $20,000-plus diamond engagement ring he bought her during the break.

Why in the world did things reverse? Because she valued herself! No longer clinging to him in desperation, she'd suddenly become exactly what he wanted: a powerful woman with her own life. The minute she embraced this, she became more valuable to him, and he could see that their relationship could be one of shared power, a vital exchange. Because she was still deeply in love with him and no longer infatuated, she could see this potential, too, and accepted his marriage proposal with loving tears.

This woman was minimizing herself, and the man she loved represented her *golden shadow,* the disowned parts of herself that she perceived to be positive. Her father and ex-husband represented the classic shadow, her disowned parts that she believed to be negative. The process we engaged in helped her learn to embrace both shadows and changed her entire outlook on life and relationships.

You can see how this process made a major difference for this one couple. Know also that if this woman goes back to her previous habit of devaluing herself, the union will revert to its old dynamics. Each person has a choice and the ultimate control to make the relationship whatever they'd love it to be.

The Divine Order of the Universe

I began to develop this method many years ago. It started when I was 17 and had just recovered from a near-death experience. I met Paul C. Bragg, an amazing and inspiring teacher, who helped me clarify my vision for my life and awaken to my dream of becoming a great teacher myself. I also saw myself as a healer and philosopher, traveling the world and setting foot in every country on the face of the earth, sharing my research findings with people who were receptive, and living an amazing and privileged life.

Of course, I didn't expect to snap my fingers and realize all of that overnight, so I decided to apply myself first to understanding the great philosophies. Not long into my studies, I was reading *Discourse on Metaphysics* by Gottfried Wilhelm Leibniz. Then 18 years old, I was struck by an overpowering idea: Leibniz believed there was a divine perfection and beauty in the universe. He wrote that there was a hidden, rational order to things, which few people were aware of and fewer still understood. As I read this, I was moved to tears of inspiration. I felt in my heart that he was sharing something profoundly true, and I dreamed of becoming one of the few who could perceive and understand the secret, sacred order of the universe.

From that moment on, it was my mission to uncover the universal principles governing this underlying structure. This exploration led me to many disciplines, including physics, astronomy, cosmology, mathematics, chemistry, theology, metaphysics, psychology, neurology, and dozens of others—all for the purpose of unveiling divine perfection.

During my early months of research, I came upon a subdiscipline of physics: quantum physics. If you've seen the film *What the Bleep Do We Know!?*, then you're already well aware of how weird, yet beautiful, the realm of quanta can be. When I was introduced to the field more than 30 years ago, I was fascinated by the mind-expanding concepts of particles and waves, collapsing wave function, and the generation and annihilation of particles. All of that may sound like pretty nerdy stuff, but when you see it in action, it just takes the lid off whatever you may have previously believed about how the universe operates. For me, this was where an intuitive leap occurred.

Quantum physicists discovered that when charged particles of matter and their complementary opposite antiparticles of antimatter collided, light emerged. When I learned this, I immediately wondered, *If two charged yet complementary opposite emotional states were to be united, could enlightenment emerge?*

This was the conception point for what you're learning in this chapter. I pondered the possibility that true science (physics) and true religion (metaphysics) were somehow the same, and both were somehow united by light.

Around that time, I was exposed to a series of texts called *The World of Mathematics*, a compilation of essays edited by James R. Newman. In the third volume's last chapter, "Mathematics as an Art," contributor John William Navin Sullivan introduced the divine proportion, also known as the golden mean, phi, the divine section, the golden cut, the golden ratio, the golden proportion, and other similar names. No matter what you call it, when it's used in architectural design, it fosters perceptions of sacred space and initiates a state of awe among those who view or enter the structure.

The earliest example of this is in the Great Pyramid of Giza, believed to be built around 2560 B.C.

Learning about this, I wondered, *Could these same awe-inspiring proportions somehow be realized in human perceptions, and could they be recognized as inherent in natural daily events?*

In the years since then, I've discovered that, yes, enlight-enment can indeed result from the unity of complementary, opposite emotional states, such as happiness and sadness, pride and humility, or anger and serenity. And, not only are sacred mathematical proportions present each day, but through a series of questions, people can observe the divine order—see an absolute balance of complementary opposites—and the result is extraordinary. In most cases, the realization of the sacred structure that exists even in their own perceptions leaves people in grateful tears with an incredible sense of personal expansion.

What You Can Expect from The Demartini Method

However beautiful this realization can be, The Demartini Method was not devised just to incite a fleeting high. I created it and have used it for years for a multitude of purposes, many of which can impact the quality of your relationships directly, and all of which have the potential to be not only mind altering but also life changing. You can extend the relatively short period of realization and mental expansion into everyday living—that's the enduring power of this method. Specifically, by using what you'll learn here, you can expect to:

- Come to love your disowned parts, integrating your own light and shadow natures

- Balance lopsided emotional perceptions

- Reconcile and dissolve conflict

- Enhance intimate communication

- Decrease blame

- Increase respect and understanding

- Dissolve remorse, bereavement, and grief over the physical death or other perceived loss of a loved one

- Experience truly unconditional love for another

- Glimpse the Grand Organized Design of your own life and relationships

The Demartini Method also enables people to access alternate states of mind. When you complete the process, you'll experience firsthand what quantum theory has hypothesized: that there are "many worlds" or "many parallel realities" accessible to you. With mental clarity, people have often experienced what quantum physicists call *nonlocality* (the principle of retained connection between any two particles that were once associated): the link between you and others who are in other spaces and times. That means you may recognize your intimate union with individuals who are alive and seem to be physically distant, or with those who are dead and seem to be metaphysically distant.

In sum, The Demartini Method allows you to awaken to the implicate order, the divine beauty, the perfection of the universe, which I sometimes call "the grand matrix."

I realize that's a huge promise. It's absolutely deliverable, but it would take an entire book to fully equip you to achieve every single one of those benefits, plus many more that are available through The Demartini Method. Indeed, I did write a book about it, and I teach weekend courses on this subject—which many of my students attend repeatedly so that they can continue to integrate what they've been learning.

There's no reason why you can't get a taste of this delicious expansion with a simple introduction to the method, however. That's what this chapter is designed to do; in addition it will show you the specific application for relationships. When you're ready to take your understanding to the next level, you can explore further with the book or weekend seminar, both of which are titled *The Breakthrough Experience* and can be accessed through my Website: **www.DrDemartini.com**.

Getting Started

The first step is to choose a subject. Pick a person whom you perceive as demonstrating your disowned parts—in other words, someone who gets under your skin, positively or negatively, inspiring either infatuation or resentment. In using The Demartini Method, you'll come to realize that you have exactly the same traits as this person, and in equal measure.

Although that notion may seem impossible to you now, I know you'll see its truth because I've worked with tens of thousands of individuals on this process. I've seen men and women reconcile and figuratively embrace those who have done seemingly irreparable harm: abandoners, rapists, molesters, attempted murderers, and others who have committed less severe crimes in the eyes of the "victims."

A participant who'd been stabbed by his mother, left for dead in a trash bin, raised by foster parents who were bearable at best and labeled "violently abusive" at worst, arrived at a place of such unconditional love for the woman who'd given birth to him that he glowed with the radiance of this realization. He came to understand the divine order in what had happened and also saw that every trait he'd imagined his mother to have existed in him in equal proportion.

In equally moving experiences, I've had the privilege of watching Holocaust survivors use this process to neutralize their feelings about Adolf Hitler. You might be wondering what would possess these elderly people to decide to even attempt this. Well, they knew that as long as they held on to these feelings, a phantom monster was still running their lives. Hitler's death hadn't released his hold on them, and they'd continue to be in his grasp until they freed themselves. So they did it.

Because they knew that they needed to remember what had happened in vivid detail, they went through a bit more hell to get to the other side; but when they completed the process, they all felt the wonderful liberation, gratitude, and expansive freedom of a personal heaven.

Given these successes, it shouldn't be too hard for you to imagine that you could embrace, for example, an ex-spouse you think has "devastated" you or a current lover who appears to be "distant and unavailable" . . . should it? From my perspective, I realize that even these comparatively small hurdles may seem enormous. I can assure you that if you give this a real chance, follow the instructions, and stay with it until your mind gives you the answers that I know reside within, you'll come to experience the same magnificence.

Actions to Create More Fulfilling Relationships

— **Choose a person as your subject for The Demartini Method.** To receive the greatest impact and most powerful transformation, choose someone who triggers the greatest feelings of repulsion/resentment (representing your shadow) or attraction/infatuation (representing your golden shadow).

Here are some questions to ask yourself to help in choosing the best subject:

- Who do I perceive to be running my life or burdening me the most?

- Who would I least like to be around?

- Who do I resent, despise, or feel repelled by the most?

- With whom am I infatuated? Who do I desire, admire, or feel attracted to the most?

- Who makes me feel "incomplete"?

- Who do I believe has "hurt" me?

- Who do I feel has left, abandoned, or dumped me?

- Who am I having difficulty loving but wish to love more?

- Who do I desire to love more fully?

It's interesting to note that the earlier someone appeared in your life and the closer they were to you, the greater their impact on you and, therefore, the more profound the domino effect will be after you've completed The Demartini

Method with this individual as your subject. If you're still having trouble choosing, go for the person who's closest to you and who was part of your life at your youngest age.

Use the following list to prompt you if you're having difficulty selecting someone.

Godfather	Godmother
Grandfather	Grandmother
Father	Mother
Stepfather	Stepmother
Father-in-law	Mother-in-law
Uncle	Aunt
Brother	Sister
Stepbrother	Stepsister
Son	Daughter
Stepson	Stepdaughter
Grandson	Granddaughter
Husband	Wife
Ex-husband	Ex-wife
Husband's friend	Wife's friend
Boyfriend	Girlfriend
Ex-boyfriend	Ex-girlfriend
Fiancé	Fiancée
Male employer	Female employer
Male employee	Female employee
Male business partner	Female business partner
Male salesperson	Female salesperson
Male teacher	Female teacher
Male student	Female student
Male colleague	Female colleague
Male ex-friend	Female ex-friend
Male rapist	Female rapist
Male incestor	Female incestor
Male litigator	Female litigator
Male killer	Female killer
Male doctor	Female doctor
Male banker	Female banker
Male accountant	Female accountant
Male lawyer	Female lawyer
Male financial consultant	Female financial consultant
Male client	Female client
Male customer	Female customer
Male patient	Female patient
Male waiter	Female waitress
Male service worker	Female service worker
Male plumber	Female plumber
Male flight attendant	Female flight attendant
Male leasing agent	Female leasing agent
Male lessee	Female lessee

Once you've selected your subject, make a copy of The Demartini Method forms, sides A and B, provided in the Appendix at the end of this book.

You'll notice that each of the two sides has seven columns. Don't let this put you off—you can do it! Anyone can, once they put their mind to it. You're ready to move on to the next chapter as soon as you've written the name of the person you've chosen on both pages of the form.

Words of Power

I empower every area of my life.

I acknowledge that I already have—in some form—what I am seeking.

I am a unique expression of all things—good and bad, happy and sad, great and small.

There is a divine perfection in the universe, and I see it.

I awaken to the implicate order, the sacred beauty, the glory of the universe.

✖✖✖ ✖✖✖

CHAPTER SIX

Instructions for Completing The Demartini Method

*For in truth great love is born of great
knowledge of the thing loved.*
— Leonardo da Vinci

Each side of The Demartini Method form has been constructed with a specific purpose in mind, as well as supporting principles. I've included the first two sides in this chapter, along with instructions so that you can go through the process just as someone would in one of my live events. You have everything you need to complete this—there are no special "tricks" to getting the results you want. It's just a matter of following instructions.

If you choose a person with whom you're primarily *infatuated*, begin your work with Side A of the form. Start with Side B if you've picked someone whom you primarily *resent*. Once you've finished the first side, complete the other.

A word of advice: Ignore the impulse to give up and declare, *Well, in my case this won't work!* That's simply not true. Don't stop once you've started. Keep going until you can sincerely answer yes to the questions that I've provided to help you determine if you're done with each column.

Giving up on this is copping out, sidelining yourself, and missing the point. You don't have to finish in five minutes; in fact, it will probably take much longer than that, maybe even several hours. You might need to take a break or a series of breaks or let it rest for a while and then come back with fresh eyes—that's fine. Just don't try to trade in one fantasy for the next or delude yourself that you can't finish this process alone and get its profound benefits. That's nonsense! You *can* do this, just as tens of thousands of others have before you.

I'm not stressing this because many people give up and don't finish. *It's not that common—in fact, it's rare.* I simply want to emphasize that it's not unusual to reach a point of fatigue or frustration, or to be overwhelmed—and that's the time to push through because the other side holds incredible insights for you.

Get inspired when you start to feel taxed by this process, because it's the moment before your breakthrough. Imagine yourself as the phoenix poised to rise out of the ashes of your old self. You're worth the effort, so let nothing stop you, not even your challenging personas with their evasive excuses. Any fatigue or resistance you might face is just your old self clinging to its disempowering illusions, fearing their transformation.

It's Worth It to Finish

Stay with the process and you'll find your heart opening wide, and you may also feel an upwelling of gratitude. In *The Breakthrough Experience* seminar programs, participants choose someone in the room who represents the individual they selected for The Demartini Method. Intuitively, they know exactly whom to pick although sometimes more than one person is chosen, as various people can be reminders of aspects of their subject. Regardless, it's always a phenomenal time in the weekend.

Some people experience the nonlocality I referred to earlier in this book: They see, feel, hear, and even smell the other person in the room with them. One young musician, who had focused on his mother, chose five women to represent her. During the session, he spoke of his gratitude, laughing through his tears and giving them all big hugs. When it was over, he told us that he'd smelled his mother's perfume and could hear her in the voices of the women who surrounded him. He announced, half-jokingly, "Hey, man, this is better than acid!"

This *can* send you where no drug ever will—to a place of lucid, unconditional love and transcendent awareness of the perfection in your own life and the wonderful gifts that every person in it brings to you. You'll know that you've completed The Demartini Method when you experience this sensation.

One particularly inspiring result comes from people who are in what I call a *relationship by default:* They realize they're not fulfilled and have let things slip into passive mediocrity. Maybe they have a "wandering eye" or have developed some other passion to substitute for what they'd really like to experience in their primary union. The bottom line is that they haven't taken any action to create what they want and instead choose to resign themselves to something they don't care about.

Keep in mind that every couple is either:

- United out of love
- Together out of choice
- Joined out of desire
- Intimate out of want
- Bound out of need
- Held out of "should"
- Tied out of "have to"

When a couple uses The Demartini Method, both partners can find a renewed sense of appreciation, gratitude, respect, and even awe for one another. They can make their way to the heart of love and be reunited there.

Love is still the greatest cure on the market—it heals all. I've watched couples at my seminars who expect to "fix" one another, but then walk away more deeply inspired about building their future than they've been for the entire duration of the relationship. One memorable pair, whom I mentioned earlier, had been married for more than 30 years when they used this method to remove an accumulation of resentments and rekindle a spark that translated into every area of their lives together—including the bedroom. What's remarkable about this isn't that it happened for them, but that I see it occur constantly with people of all ages, backgrounds, and lifestyles.

If any of this sounds like what you'd love to have in your life, then get started! There's no need to go through the exercise prior to plunging in, but be sure you've read this chapter up to this point, as well as the previous one. Then just put a copy of Side A or B in front of you and follow the instructions on the next few pages.

Side A

Note: A copy of the form used for this exercise is included in the Appendix. Here are guidelines for using it:

This part of The Demartini Method is designed to neutralize your infatuation with someone by helping you:

- Identify the traits you admire or perceive as positive

- Acknowledge their existence within you

- See how each one can actually be a drawback

- Realize that the counter traits are also present and are acted out by others

- Recognize what benefits might occur if this individual were to magically behave in the opposite way

This will bring balance to your relationship with that person and to your life as a whole.

Column 1

— *Purpose:* To pinpoint the specific, most positively charged human traits, actions, or inactions that draw or attract you to this person—the ones that "hook" you and/or bring out a "positive" emotional feeling of admiration or infatuation.

— *Supporting principle:* Human beings have every trait, as well as its opposite. All characteristics can be summarized and concisely written down into a brief phrase of one to four words.

— *Instructions:* Starting in Column 1, "Trait I most like or admire about him or her," use just a few words (no more than four for each quality) to list what you value and believe to be the most positive. For example, you could write *nice hair, made me smile,* or *gentle.* You'll write only one quality in each space provided in the first column, so allow yourself enough room.

The primary question to ask yourself as you complete Column 1 is: **What human trait, action, or inaction do I most like, admire, or consider positive or attractive about this person?** This could be from the temporal categories (past, present, or potential future) and from any of the seven areas of life. In other words, reflect on what you like in spiritual, mental, vocational, financial, familial, social, and physical terms. If you can't think of something that's happening right now, look into the past or project into the future.

Here are some other ways to ask this principal question:

- **Why is this person likable?**

- **What has he or she done or not done that made me feel good?**

- **Why do I seek and admire this person?**

- **Why do I feel positive when I think of this individual?**

- **Why can't I be away from him or her?**

- **Why do I want to deal with this person or see him or her again?**

- **Why do I desire this person so much?**

Clearly and precisely define the human character trait, action, or inaction you *most* like, admire, or consider positive or attractive about this person. As you write, concentrate on the exact time (when) and space (where, that is, the location in terms of direction and distance) the person expressed this. The more detailed you are, the more useful it will be. Generalities slow down the process, but specifics speed it up.

— *Confirm that you're done:* Ask yourself, *Are there any more human traits, actions, or inactions that I most like, admire, or consider positive or attractive about this person?*

Column 2

— *Purposes:* To reawaken and capture specific memories where others have seen you display this same or similar characteristic, action, or inaction in one or many forms and to an equal degree; to help you realize that people are aware of your expression of this trait and that whatever you see in them is truly reflected in your own life in some way; to dissolve any infatuation you might have toward the individual that you're using as a subject; and to elevate and balance the minimized or self-depreciative and sacrificed part of yourself.

— *Supporting principles:* Human beings have every trait, as well as its opposite. **Don't bother questioning whether you have this quality, because you do. It's not a matter of *if* you possess it, but only *where, when,* and *who* has seen it.**

All characteristics are apparent to someone.

You never gain or lose traits; you only change their form, and your hierarchy of values determines how they're expressed.

Everyone is your reflection: The seer, the seeing, and the seen are the same. In less lofty terms, if you spot it in them, you've got it in you.

— *Instructions:* Go to Column 2, "Initials of people who see this trait in me." In the space next to each positive trait you listed in Column 1, write as many initials as you can, and don't worry about making them legible. As you fill the space, write over the original initials with new ones. The box may become black with ink—it doesn't matter if you can't read it. The point is to acknowledge that others have seen this trait in you. One person may have noticed it many times; others may have seen it once or more. (But don't just write *everybody,* because that's an illusion. Be specific. This is a way of integrating your brain and your personas.)

As you complete Column 2, ask yourself the following: **Who observes(ed) or recognizes(ed) this human trait in me, in a form/expression either similar to or different from this person's?** It's not a matter of whether you have this, but only a question of *where, when,* and *in what form* it's been noticed by another. For example, if you've written *gave me money,* this doesn't mean that you must have delivered sacks of gold to someone. Who perceives you as being generous with cash or giving something of monetary worth?

Here are additional ways to ask this primary question:

- **Where and when have I had this character trait, and who's seen it?**

- **Where and when have I exhibited this attribute and others were positively affected by it? Who's witnessed that?**

- **Who's seen me act out this quality? Who else?**

Continue until you can honestly see that you demonstrate this trait to the same degree as the person in question, although it may be in different forms. If you're not completely convinced that you have this characteristic in some regard and to an equal extent, then keep writing more initials until you are. This is called truly "owning your golden shadow." Through this process, you reclaim your disowned parts that you believe are positive. This could take anywhere from 10 to 50 initials.

Be sure you identify and include who observes the trait in you now; otherwise, you might fall into the illusion that you once had it but you don't anymore.

— *Confirm that you're done:* Ask yourself, *Can I see that I have this human trait, action, or inaction in a similar or different form, and to exactly the same degree, as I observe it in the other person?*

Column 3

— *Purpose:* To further dissolve any remaining infatuation with the person, and to neutralize any admiration for the character trait itself.

— *Supporting principles:* Every human trait has two sides, a benefit and a drawback; nothing is one-sided. Everything is neutral until someone judges whether or not it's beneficial, according to his or her hierarchy of values.

When we're infatuated with others, we tend to inject their belief system into our lives and try to change ourselves to be more like them.

— *Instructions:* Move on to Column 3, "How this trait in him or her is a drawback or disservice to me." Write down the abbreviations of the word(s) that represent how the quality, action, or inaction from Column 1 hinders or hindered you (or disserves or disserved you) in all seven areas of life, as well as in the past, present, and future. For example, if you listed *considerate* in Column 1, the Column 3 disadvantages might be that this person's consideration is time-consuming, obligating, and distracting; it fosters expectations, dependency, and infatuation; and it may have a hidden agenda. To save space, these could be abbreviated to something like this: *TC, Obl., Dist., Exp., Dep., Inf., HA.* Shorten your terms in a way that makes sense to you.

The primary question to ask yourself as you complete Column 3 is: **How is the trait I listed in Column 1 a drawback or disservice to me as it's expressed by this person?**

Here are more ways to ask yourself this:

- **How did or does this characteristic obstruct me? How else?**

- **How is what this person did or didn't do a curse to me?**

- **What shortcomings did I observe or receive from the individual expressing this trait?**

- **How or in what way could this attribute impede me?**

- **How could his or her action or inaction impact me negatively?**

Keep writing until you dissolve any admiration or infatuation toward this trait—until you feel neutral about it, and you can see that it has equal benefits and drawbacks. This generally requires at least 15 abbreviated downsides—and often more.

— *Confirm that you're done:* Ask yourself, *Can I see that this trait in him or her has both positive and negative aspects?*

Column 4

— *Purpose:* To dissolve any pride associated with expressing the trait listed in Column 1.

— *Supporting principles:* Elevated pride draws tragedy, challenge, humbling circumstances, and distracting low priorities into our lives.

Everyone displays every trait and its opposite at the same time and to the same degree, such as being generous and stingy, nice and mean, or considerate and inconsiderate.

All qualities have two sides, a benefit and a drawback; no trait is one-sided.

— *Instructions:* Now go to Column 4, "How this trait in me is a drawback or disservice to others." Abbreviate the word(s) representing how your particular expression of the attribute listed in Column 1 hinders or hindered others who saw it in you.

The primary question to ask yourself as you complete Column 3 is: **How is the trait I listed in Column 1 a drawback or disservice to others as it's expressed by me?** Another way to ask this is: **How has acting out my matching characteristic disadvantaged others?**

Keep writing until you dissolve any admiration or infatuation toward this trait in yourself—until you neutralize the pride that you may have had about it. Be mindful of how this can be an obstacle in all seven areas of life. This also generally requires 15 or more abbreviated drawbacks, so write small to allow yourself as much room as possible.

— *Confirm that you're done:* Ask yourself, *Can I see that this trait in me has been both a service and a disservice, a blessing and a curse, to others?*

Column 5

— *Purposes:* To dissolve whatever "all" or "none" and "always" or "never" illusions and labels you may have associated with the person who's the subject of this exercise; to open the doorway to greater communication with that individual.

— *Supporting principle:* Human beings equally display every trait and its opposite.

— *Instructions:* Go to Column 5, "Initials of those who see in him or her the opposite trait to Column 1." Write the initials of individuals who perceive the person in question as having Column 1's "anti-trait"—the opposite of what you wrote there. Be sure that if the quality listed in Column 1 (for example, *nice*) is directed from the person in question to a particular individual (for example, your brother), then the people you note as seeing the opposite trait *(mean)* know that it's directed toward the same person (your brother), thereby making the method "vector or person specific." In other words, take the time to realize how opposites can be seen within the exact same relationship. This way you can neutralize the lopsided label that you've place on this dynamic. However, if the characteristic is general and not directed toward anyone in particular, then simply identify the people who see the opposite in your subject.

The key question to ask yourself as you complete Column 5 is: **Who observes(ed) or recognizes(ed) the exact opposite trait in him or her, and to what degree?** (Be vector specific if applicable.)

The following are alternative ways to ask yourself this:

- **Where and when does this person possess the opposite character trait, the anti-trait, and who's seen it?**

- **Where is this person the opposite of what I admire? Who sees him or her in this way?**

Keep writing down initials until you can truly sense that there's a perfect balance of the trait and its opposite, or anti-trait, and that there are plenty of people who verify this.

— *Confirm that you're done:* Ask yourself, *Can I see that this person has both sides (trait and anti-trait) equally? Can I acknowledge that he or she acts one way when I support his or her core beliefs and the opposite way when I challenge them? If I learn how to communicate effectively in accordance with this person's higher values, can I now understand that I could experience different outcomes?*

Column 6

— *Purposes:* To expand your awareness of the equal and opposite action, inaction, or characteristic that is simultaneously occurring whenever the person in question is expressing the admired trait; to acquaint you with the hidden intelligence and balancing order that's present among all actions and events in the life matrix; to become humbled to the Grand Organized Design.

— *Supporting principles:* Nothing is ever missing—it simply exists in a form that's not being recognized or acknowledged. All human beings receive a complementary balance of traits from others and within themselves in order to maintain a loving equilibrium; realizing this is "the great discovery."

— *Instructions:* Go to Column 6, "Initials of people who simultaneously did/do the opposite trait to Column 1." Write the initials of whoever was acting out, in the exact same moment, the opposite attribute to the one you listed in Column 1. Again, be vector specific. If the person was nice, considerate, or generous to your brother, for instance, who was observed being mean, inconsiderate, and stingy toward him at the same time? Your answers may include one or many people, male or female, close or distant, real or imagined. If you can recall one side of something, you always have the power to come up with the other angle. Human perception demands such simultaneous contrasts.

As you complete Column 6, ask: **Who is or was acting out the trait opposite to the one in Column 1 at the exact same moment?**

Some other ways to ask this primary question are the following:

- **Who is or was acting out the opposite human trait to the one I like or liked at the exact same moment? Who else?**

- **When this person was positive, accepting, and admiring to me, who was simultaneously negative, rejecting, or critical of me?**

Repeat this step for every instance that you can remember someone acting out this opposite quality, until you can't think of any more times.

— *Confirm that you're done:* Ask yourself, *Can I see that there has been simultaneous expression of this trait and its opposite on every occasion?*

Column 7

— *Purposes:* To dissolve any "nightmares" concerning the person's expression of the trait opposite to the one you've admired; to indirectly dissolve any remaining infatuation with the admired property in Column 1.

— *Supporting principles:* Everything has two sides, a benefit and a drawback; nothing is one-sided.

Every aspect of life is neutral until someone judges whether or not it's beneficial, according to his or her hierarchy of values.

— Instructions: Finish Side A with Column 7, "Benefits that I experience when this person acts out the opposite trait to Column 1." Write down the blessings, the upside, and the benefits to you if the person were to act out the opposite of what you wrote in Column 1.

The paramount question to ask as you complete this column is: **If this person acted out the opposite human trait to the one I wrote in Column 1, what would the benefit be to me?** Another way to ask this question is: **What would the advantage be if this person acted differently than I'd like?**

List abbreviations of the benefits and keep writing until you no longer feel infatuated with the person's expression of the trait in Column 1, and you're not dreading or having nightmares about them being the opposite.

— Confirm that you're done: Ask yourself, *Can I clearly see the benefits to me if this person were to demonstrate the opposite trait?*

Side B

Note: A copy of the form used for this exercise is included in the Appendix. Here are guidelines for using it:

This part of The Demartini Method is designed to neutralize your resentments toward someone by helping you do the following:

- Identify the traits you perceive as negative.

- Acknowledge their existence in you.

- See how each one can actually serve you and others.

- Realize that the counter qualities are also present and being acted out by others.

- Recognize what drawbacks might occur if this person were to magically behave in the opposite way.

Column 8

— *Purpose:* To pinpoint the specific, most negatively charged human traits, actions, or inactions that push you away from or repel you from this person—the ones that "hook" you and/or bring out a "negative" emotional feeling of loathing or resentment.

— *Supporting principle:* Human beings have every trait, as well as its opposite. All characteristics can be summarized and concisely written down into a brief phrase of one to four words.

— *Instructions:* Starting in Column 8, "Trait I dislike or despise most about him or her," use just a few words (no more than four for each one) to list the qualities you despise and believe to be the most negative. For example, you could write *lazy* or *never repays loans* or *lies*. You'll put only one trait in each space provided in this column, so allow yourself enough room.

The primary question to ask as you complete Column 8 is: **What human trait, action, or inaction do I most dislike, despise, or consider negative or repulsive about this person?** This could be from the past, present, or potential future and from any of the seven areas of life. In other words, reflect on what you dislike in spiritual, mental, vocational, financial, familial, social, and physical terms. Also consider temporal categories: If you can't think of something that's happening right now, look into the past or project into the future.

Here are some other ways to ask this question:

- What makes him or her unlikable?

- What has this person done or not done that feels so bad?

- What characteristic does this person demonstrate that angers me?

- What can't I like about him or her?

- What is it that makes me avoid and despise him or her?

- Why do I hurt when I think about this person?

- Why can't I be near this individual?

- Why don't I want to deal with this person or see him or her again?

- What has this person done or not done that I think I haven't or have done?

- Why can't I stand him or her?

- What negative quality does this person possess that blocks me from loving him or her?

Clearly and precisely define the human character trait, action, or inaction that you *most* dislike. As you write, concentrate on the exact time (when) and space (where, that is, the location in terms of direction and distance) the person expressed this. The more detailed you are, the more useful it will be. Generalities slow down the process, but specifics speed it up.

— *Confirm that you're done:* Ask yourself, *Are there any more human traits, actions, or inactions that I dislike, despise, or consider negative or repulsive about this person?*

Column 9

— *Purposes:* To reawaken and capture specific memories where others have seen you express this same or similar trait, action, or inaction in one or many forms and to an equal degree; to help you realize that people are aware of your expression of this trait and that whatever you see in them is truly reflected in your own life in some way; to dissolve any resentment you might have toward the individual whom you're using as a subject; to lower and balance the exaggerated or self-aggrandized and inflated part of yourself.

— *Supporting principles:* Human beings have every characteristic, as well as its opposite. **Don't bother questioning whether you have this trait, because you do. It's not a matter of *if* you have it, but only *where, when,* and *who* has seen it.** All qualities are apparent to someone.

You never gain or lose anything; you only change the forms. Your hierarchy of values determines how your attributes are expressed.

Everyone is your reflection: The seer, the seeing, and the seen are the same. In less lofty terms, if you spot it in them, you've got it in you.

— *Instructions:* Go to Column 9, "Initials of people who see this trait in me." In the space next to each positive trait you listed earlier, write as many initials as you can and don't worry about making them legible. As you fill the space, write over the original letters with new ones. The box may become black with ink, but it doesn't matter if you can't read it. The point is to acknowledge that others have seen this trait in you. One person may have seen it many times; others may have noticed it once or more. (But don't just write *everybody,* because that's an illusion—be specific. This is a way of integrating your brain and your personas.)

As you complete Column 9, ask yourself the following: **Who observes(ed) or recognizes(ed) this human trait in me, in a form/expression either similar to or different from this person's?** It's not a matter of whether you have this, but only a question of *where, when,* and *in what form* it's been observed by another person. For example, if you've written *stole money from me,* this doesn't mean that you must have literally robbed someone. Who perceives you as having cheated them or taken money or something of value without permission?

Here are additional ways to ask this primary question:

- **Where and when have I had this characteristic, and who's seen it?**

- **Where and when have I had this trait that others feel pained by, and who's noticed it?**

- **Who's observed me act this out? Who else?**

Continue until you can honestly see that you demonstrate this trait to the same degree as the person in question, although it may be in different forms. If you're not completely convinced that you have this attribute in some regard and to an equal extent, then keep writing more initials until you are. This is called truly "integrating your shadow." Through this process, you reclaim your disowned parts that you believe are negative. This could take anywhere between 10 and 50 initials.

Be sure that you identify and include those who observe the trait in you *now;* otherwise, you might fall into the illusion that you once had the trait but don't anymore.

— *Confirm that you're done:* Ask yourself, *Can I see that I have this trait, action, or inaction in a similar or different form and to exactly the same degree as I observe it in the other person?*

Column 10

— *Purpose:* To further dissolve any remaining resentment toward the person, and to neutralize any contempt or fear of the characteristic itself.

— *Supporting principles:* Everything has two sides, a benefit and a drawback; nothing is one-sided.

Every trait is neutral until someone judges whether or not it's beneficial, according to his or her hierarchy of values. When we disapprove of others, we tend to project our belief systems into their lives and try to change them to be more like us.

— *Instructions:* Move on to Column 10, "How this trait in him or her is a benefit or service to me." Think about words that represent how the property in Column 8 helps or helped you (or serves or served you) in all seven areas of life, as well as in the past, present, and future. For example, if you had listed *inconsiderate* in Column 8, the Column 10 benefits might be that this person's lack of consideration frees up your time, doesn't incur obligations, is liberating, creates no expectations, and keeps you from building a fantasy about him or her. To save space, these advantages could be abbreviated something like this: *FT, No Obl., Lib., No Exp., No Fant.*

The primary question to ask yourself as you complete Column 10 is: **How is the human trait I listed in Column 8 a benefit or service to me as it's expressed by this person?**

The following questions are some other ways to ask this:

- **How did this characteristic serve me? How else?**

- **What could be the blessing of what this person did or didn't do?**

- **What advantages did I observe or receive from the individual expressing this trait?**

- **How did this person's action or inaction impact me positively?**

Keep writing until you dissolve any resentment toward or fear of the person and this trait—until you feel neutral and can see that he or she has both benefits and drawbacks. This generally requires at least 15 or more abbreviated benefits.

— *Confirm that you're done:* Ask yourself, *Can I see that his or her trait has been equally a service and a disservice, a blessing and a curse?*

Column 11

— *Purpose:* To dissolve any shame or guilt associated with expressing the trait listed in Column 8.

— *Supporting principles:* All humans display every trait and its opposite at the same time and to the same degree, such as being generous and stingy, nice and mean, and considerate and inconsiderate.

All traits have two sides, a benefit and a drawback; no trait is one-sided.

— *Instructions:* Now go to Column 11, "How this trait in me is a benefit or service to others." Abbreviate the word(s) representing how your particular expression of the trait listed in Column 8 benefits or serves others who see it in you.

The primary question to ask as you complete Column 11 is: **How is the trait I listed in Column 8 a benefit or service to others as it's expressed by me?** Another way to ask this is: **How is my matching characteristic a benefit to those who see me that way?**

Continue writing until you dissolve any resentment or hatred of this quality in yourself. Keep in mind how it can be an advantage in all seven areas of life. This again generally requires at least 15 or more abbreviated benefits, so write small to allow yourself as much room as possible.

— *Confirm that you're done:* Ask yourself, *Can I see that this trait in me has been both a service and a disservice, a blessing and a curse?*

Column 12

— *Purposes:* To dissolve whatever "all" or "none" and "always" or "never" illusions and labels that you may have associated with the person who's the subject of this exercise; to open the doorway to greater communication with that individual.

— *Supporting principle:* Humans equally display every trait and its opposite.

— *Instructions:* Go to Column 12, "Initials of people who see in him or her the opposite trait to Column 8." Write the initials of individuals who perceive the person in question as having Column 8's "anti-trait" (the opposite of what you wrote there). Be sure that if the quality listed in Column 8 (for example, *mean*) is directed from the person in question to a particular individual (for example, your brother), then the people you note as seeing the opposite trait *(nice)* know that it's directed toward the same person (your brother), thereby making the method vector specific. In other words, take the time to realize how opposites can be seen in the exact same relationship. This way you can neutralize the lopsided label that you've placed on this dynamic. However, if the trait is general, then simply identify the people who see its opposite.

The key question to ask as you complete this column is: **Who observes(ed) or recognizes(ed) the exact opposite** human trait in him or her, and to the same degree? (Be vector specific if applicable.)

Here are more ways to ask this:

- **Where and when does this person possess the opposite characteristic, the anti-trait, and who's seen it?**

- **Where is the individual the opposite of what I resent? Who sees him or her in this way?**

Keep writing initials until you can truly sense that there's a perfect balance of the attribute and its opposite, and that there are plenty of people who verify this.

— *Confirm that you're done:* Ask yourself, *Can I see that this person has both sides (trait and anti-trait) equally? Can I acknowledge that the subject acts one way when I support his or her core beliefs and the opposite way when I challenge them? If I learned how to communicate effectively in accordance with this person's higher values, can I now realize that I could experience different outcomes?*

Column 13

— *Purposes:* To expand your awareness of the equal and opposite action, inaction, or characteristic that simultaneously occurs whenever the person in question expresses the resented trait; to acquaint you with the hidden intelligence and balancing order that's present among all actions and events in the life matrix; to become humbled to the Grand Organized Design.

— *Supporting principles:* Nothing is ever missing—it simply exists in a form that's not being recognized or acknowledged.

All humans receive a complementary balance of traits from others and within themselves in order to maintain a loving equilibrium—realizing this is "the great discovery."

— *Instructions:* Go to Column 13, "Initials of people who simultaneously did/do the opposite trait to Column 8." Write the initials of whoever was acting out, in that exact same moment, the opposite of what you listed in Column 8. Again, be vector specific. If the person was mean, inconsiderate, or stingy with your brother, for instance, then who was observed being nice, considerate, and generous toward him at the same time? Your answers may include one or many people, male or female, close or distant, real or imagined. If you can recall one side of the story, you always have the power to come up with the other. Human perception demands such simultaneous contrasts.

As you complete Column 13, ask: **Who is or was acting out the human trait opposite to the one in Column 8 at the exact same moment?** (Again, be vector specific if applicable.)

Here are additional ways to ask this primary question:

- **Who is or was acting out the opposite trait to the one I dislike(d) at the exact same moment? Who else?**

- **When this person was negative, rejecting, and critical of me, who was simultaneously positive, accepting, or praising me?**

Repeat this step for every instance that you can remember this person displaying this opposite attribute until you can't think of anymore.

— *Confirm that you're done:* Ask yourself, *Can I see that there's been simultaneous expression of this trait and its opposite on every occasion?*

While researching thousands of cases of synchronicity, I came upon another amazing component of "the great discovery": During conversations with friends, you won't find yourself discussing any imagined happy future without at the same time attracting others into your space or sphere of awareness who will have you simultaneously talking about the counterbalancing, past disasters. This holds true for future nightmares and past fantasies as well. In other words, you and your friends make up parts of a living matrix that keeps you ever present (in the now).

If you're reminiscing about the "good old days" (past fantasies) with a group, don't be surprised if your partner emerges or walks by at that very moment to let you know that if you don't get off your butt and go to work, the bills won't be paid in the future (nightmare). Similarly, if you're recalling the "bad old days" (past nightmares or perceived failures), don't be alarmed if your mate appears to let you know that you can do it and that he or she has confidence in your capabilities.

If you're focused on the past, you'll attract people to neutralize you in time to redirect you toward the future— all in order to keep you ever present. Your memories and projections are actually inseparable and helping you stay truly in the now.

You also won't have someone attempt to put space constraints on you without simultaneously having another attempt to liberate you. Again, this means that you and others make up parts of a living matrix that keeps you grounded.

Finally, you'll remain in equilibrium and be present (here/now) in space-time throughout your life, although you may not be conscious of it. Remember that there's nothing but the presence of love, and all else is illusion.

Column 14

— *Purposes:* To dissolve any fantasies concerning the person's expression of the trait opposite to the one you've despised; to indirectly dissolve any remaining resentment of the disliked quality in Column 8.

— *Supporting principles:* Everything has two sides, a benefit and a drawback; nothing is one-sided. Every trait is neutral until someone judges whether or not it's beneficial, according to his or her hierarchy of values.

— *Instructions:* Finish Side B with Column 14, "Drawbacks to me of this person acting out the opposite trait to Column 8." Now you're going to write down the curse, the downside, and the drawbacks to you if the person were to act out the opposite of what you wrote in Column 8.

The foremost question to ask as you complete Column 14 is: **If this person acted out the opposite of what I wrote in Column 8, what would the drawback be to me?** Another way to ask this question is: **What would the disadvantage be if this person were the way I wish him or her to be?**

List the abbreviations of the drawbacks, and keep writing until you no longer feel resentful about the person's expression of the trait in Column 8, and you're not wishing for or having fantasies about him or her being the opposite.

— *Confirm that you're done:* Ask yourself, *Can I clearly see the drawbacks to me if this person were to demonstrate the opposite attribute?*

There's More

The Demartini Method also includes a Side C, which is designed to neutralize a trait, action, or inaction you perceive to have been gained or lost, such as when you start a relationship and delude yourself that this new person "brings" some unfamiliar quality to your life, or when you've ended a partnership and you feel that your ex has "taken away" something that you'll miss. Instructions for Side C appear in a later chapter, and the form is in the Appendix.

(There are also Sides D and E, which are outside the scope of this book but can be accessed through advanced training with the Concourse of Wisdom School of Philosophy and Healing. For more information about this, please visit my Website, **www.DrDemartini.com**.)

If you find that you're struggling through this process and have questions, please turn to the section Objections Frequently Posed about The Demartini Method in the Appendix.

What You Can Expect When You're Finished

How will you know when you've truly completed The Demartini Method? I regularly see the same signs in people as they finish. The most immediate and noticeable one is a feeling of weightlessness and gratitude. You may find yourself welling up and experiencing any or all of the following:

— **Tears of inspiration.** People cry when they're moved. This isn't polarized emotion but synthesized love. These aren't sobs of sadness or happiness; they're tears of gratitude and love.

— **Growth in self-love.** Every time you care for someone more fully, you increase your self-worth. This is a real and spiritual experience of grace and communion with your soul— you feel what some call "the hand of God" on your shoulder.

— **Unconditional gratitude.** You become suffused with thankfulness for every completed aspect of the subject. There's nothing you can perceive that doesn't deserve your thanks—you feel true gratitude for this person just as he or she is, with no conditions. You'd like to say, "Thank you for being who you are."

— **Unconditional love.** You now have an unshakable depth of affection for this person. You feel the inner unity in the outer duality of two people, observing it as literally true instead of figuratively. You're in the highest state of the human psyche, swimming in the *vesica pisces*—the place of divine revelation and creation, of unconditional love.

— **Fearlessness and guiltlessness.** There's no impulse to apologize, seek, or confer forgiveness. You've shed the lopsided beliefs of fear and guilt that induce such responses.

— **Speechlessness and outward silence.** There's a point where there's nothing to be said, and all that remains is to embrace the person you love. The last words before the truth of silence are "Thank you" and "I love you."

— **Reduced mind chatter.** Brain noise normally fills your consciousness, but in this state, it dissipates. The amount of jabbering is directly proportional to how many fragmented personas you have inside (how many parts of you have been disowned). The more clear your awareness, the less they have to say. When you've completed the process, the only voice left is that of your enlightened soul, and this part of you requires few if any words.

— **Balance, centeredness, and integration.** Your power rises as you integrate the formerly fragmented parts of yourself. You become balanced, your physiology normalizes, and you heal.

— **Lightness and weightlessness.** You may feel that you've finally lifted a burden, and in a way you have: You've released your disowned parts from the bondage of your polarized emotions. Some people have actually lost physical weight from this process, because a strong component of gaining pounds is emotional. Decrease the charge and reduce the weight.

— **Nonlocal, all-sense presence of the loved one.** In this state of mental clarity and centeredness, you can access anybody, alive or dead, at any time and place. This is the mystical, the Christ or Buddha, experience; indeed, it's "better than acid."

— **Experience of light.** When you become fully openhearted, you may have the unforgettable experience of light. If you do this in the presence of others, they'll be able to see your radiance, too. I hope you reach this state at least once, so you'll know the truth of your spiritual illumination.

— **Certainty of truth.** You know with absolute clarity and unshakable confidence that you truly love the person. You recognize that there's one great truth: The universe is filled with love, and all else is an illusion.

— **Desire to embrace.** You feel irresistibly drawn to the person because your resentment that normally keeps people out is gone. The walls have come down, all fear is gone, and you have an overwhelming urge to embrace the loved one, not because of any infatuation, but as a result of the oneness of reflection.

— **Uplifted head and eyes.** Having done this process in more than 50 countries around the world, I've seen one thing happen everywhere I go: People raise their eyes as if they're looking to something greater above and beyond. You look up and say, "Thank you, universe," because you realize that before this moment, you didn't understand how beautifully it was ordered.

— **Domino effect of a fuller understanding of past events.** Everything begins to make sense: Your history seems precisely balanced and orchestrated to create today. You make connections between the cause-and-effect patterns of life, fascinated to find out that it has all unfolded perfectly.

These are the predictable results of what I regard as a scientific ritual. If you complete the process, you will, without a doubt, experience some or all of this. It's a powerful encounter with your soul that has far-reaching effects. Your buttons become less "pushable." When you observe a behavior that might have gotten under your skin in the past, you may find yourself calm and confident instead. Likewise, you'll be able to move more gracefully through infatuation, recognizing it for what it is and choosing to take the relationship to a plane of fulfillment instead of illusory fantasy.

As you complete this method with more people, your wisdom grows: You become adept at finding symmetry and balance in your illusions; and feel gratitude, love, certainty, and spirit each time the lightbulb goes on. If you're enlightened, your consciousness embraces the universe and the people in it. You become a worthy mirror of your soul.

Beyond this, if you'd love to experience the presence not only of your spirit, but also of your soul mate, you're now poised to do so with an open heart. In the next chapter, these special partners are revealed, explained, and made available to you immediately. Once you've completed The Demartini Method even once, you're more ready than ever before to experience this intimate connection.

Actions to Create More Fulfilling Relationships

— **Use The Demartini Method.** Complete the process at least once in the next few days, setting aside a couple of hours to really work through this and achieve the results you want. Follow the instructions and stay with it until you get to the other side.

— **And remember** . . . Yes! You *can* complete this process. Allow yourself no excuses and keep going, no matter what! Simply think of and write down the "most" pleasing (liked) and displeasing (disliked) attributes. Isolate the specific moments when the person expressed these traits in order to recapture your emotions. Find your reflection of them, to the same degree, in some form.

Embrace your disowned traits. If you spot them in someone else, you've got them in you. Everyone has *every* quality, including you.

You neither gain nor lose anything throughout your life; you only change its form. Everything is conserved through space-time.

Don't even think that you don't have a trait to the same degree as someone else. Keep looking for those who see you with it. Confirm that the person has the opposite quality to the same degree (50-50). Everyone has a perfect blend of complementary properties.

For every liked (positive) characteristic, there are many equilibrating drawbacks, and vice versa. All traits have positive and negative aspects.

Don't stop writing benefits until you feel balanced and grateful and can honestly say, "I thank God that this person has this trait," "I have no desire to change him or her," and "I hope my child has this." Keep following the process until you love and appreciate this person, you feel his or her presence, and he or she appears to you in some form.

Words of Power

I get inspired when I face obstacles in life.

I know that when I am most challenged,
I am about to break through.

There is nothing but love, and all else is illusion.

I am a human being with every trait serving
me in perfect balance.

Whatever appears, I look for its other side.

I am a master of The Demartini Method and of love.

❈❈❈ ❈❈❈

CHAPTER SEVEN

The Real Story on Finding Your Soul Mate

*I made you take time to look at what I saw, and when you
took time to really notice my flower, you hung all your associations
with flowers on my flower, and you write about my flower as
if I think and see what you think and see—and I don't.*
— Georgia O'Keeffe

"**B**e yourself." Your mother and anyone else who's ever counseled you on love have probably told you this. It's straightforward advice that most of us take as useless, empty flattery, as in "You're great just the way you are, and if people don't recognize that, they're fools." Yeah, okay. Thanks, Mom.

Until you're ready to look deeper, such advice can seem impractical: *Be myself? What does that mean? Don't wear makeup? Belch at the table? Tell someone all about my last crummy relationship and then yawn when they say something that I find boring? I don't think so.*

All right, I get it—you want to put your "best" foot forward when you're meeting people and developing connections. That's great. And once you're in a relationship, there are some social conventions that you might agree to continue to observe. But let's dive below the surface: If you'd truly love to "find" and create a lasting bond with a soul mate, and not just have a few dates (or decades of wedded mediocrity), it's best to start with yourself.

Examining your inner self means acknowledging what you've read throughout this book and what you've experienced, too, if you completed the exercises from the previous chapters. There's *nothing* missing from your life. **You encompass all things, and so does everyone else.** You're a microcosm of the infinite, expressing this limitless potentiality in a particular human, finite form directed by your unique set of values. You're kind and cruel, generous and greedy, boring and exciting, and so on—one and the other for as far as the mind can reach.

If you're single and want to be with that "special someone," you might find yourself thinking that you'd prefer it if I got down to business. Why don't I just tell you how to get the universe to cough up the man or woman of your dreams?

If you're without a mate and unhappy, take this as an opportunity to exercise your insight and patience. Remember that trying to "get" or "find" someone or something in life is futile, but it's a sign of maturity and wisdom when you prepare for a loving connection by realizing your own wholeness. That's your first step—not scouting the best bars or ramming your shopping cart into good-looking prospects at the grocery store. When you focus on yourself first, you can walk into a relationship empowered and aware of your own fullness, instead of being driven by a sense of need or desperation. A soul mate isn't someone who gives you what you lack, but instead is a person who can share your life, for whatever period of time. Together, you can explore something magical that transcends comparing similarities and differences and enters into the realm of true love.

Movies and fairy tales aside, the great beauty of recognizing a soul mate isn't the moment of "You complete me," so much as "You see me." That could be short for *You see me in my entirety, including what you perceive as good and bad, and you appreciate all of it. You love me for every facet—not just the parts that I think are "acceptable" to show the world, but for the complete depth and breadth of my soul.*

Examine my answers to these questions as you begin to focus on your inner self:

- What are loving relationships? *Ones that help you see yourself.*

- Who attracts them? *People who care for themselves.*

- Where do you discover bonds of affection? *Within yourself.*

- How do you find lasting connections? *By being yourself.*

When you're being true to your heart and to what you love, you increase the probability of attracting those who are also committed to living in that manner. You can know the real person instead of falling for a facade, and in turn, be cherished for who *you* really are. When you appreciate that you and others have a balance of all traits, actions, and inactions and that their forms are determined by each individual's values, then you can set reasonable expectations, which is essential to initiating steadfast and loving relationships.

Finding Your Soul Mate Right Now

In my seminars, I meet plenty of people who are seeking soul mates, hoping to find that special someone who will "fulfill their destiny." I also talk to couples who feel that whatever spark that once burned between them has died, and they want to revive it or get out.

In either case, I use the same process. For example, if a woman feels that she'd dearly love to have a new man in her life, I'll ask her to describe this fellow.

She might say, "I'd love to be involved with someone who's kind, wise, funny, creative, family oriented, financially successful, generous, and handsome."

The list could go on for much longer, but we'll start here. So, I'd then inquire, "Who in your life exemplifies kindness to you right now?"

There's certainly someone: a friend, relative, colleague, client, or mentor—a specific person who's already exhibiting this trait to her on a regular basis. Next, I'd ask her to identify those who demonstrate each of the attributes she's looking for, being detailed and listing as many people as she can for each one.

You can see where this is headed: It will soon become apparent to her that what she's seeking has already been abundantly supplied. Just as she encompasses all traits, so do those around her, and the features that she thinks are attractive currently exist in her life, displayed in the form of many people instead of just one. *Her soul mate will have already manifested in her life, surrounding her with the qualities that she cherishes.*

Of course, in addition to all the admirable or "positive" things she might be looking for, there will also be their complementary opposites or "negative" traits. These will be demonstrated or exhibited by one or many individuals in her life to synchronistically maintain the ever-present and soulful harmony. Beware of seeking one-sided mates, for this will be futile. It's wiser to honor nature's law of balance in your expectations and dreams.

So, the next question would be, "If you could have this all in one person, would you really want that? Because the universe conserves its perfect proportion through time and space. If you have all these 'good' things in the form of one, then it's likely that the many will disperse. Is that truly your desire?"

Her answer could be yes or no. You might be surprised how many times this one query causes someone to rethink his or her position: *Do I really want these traits all in one person, or do I like that I have multiple representations of this already in my world?*

One woman, a high-end interior designer I met in Hollywood several years ago, provides an interesting case study. To be blunt, she told me that she was horny, frustrated, and ready for a new relationship. "Dr. Demartini, I need a man," she said. "I really want a guy in my life."

"I don't think so," I replied, "or else you'd be dating someone. Let's take a look at what your life's demonstrating and get clear on your values."

As we examined this together, she realized that the last time she'd been romantically involved with someone, her business had nearly gone under, she'd almost sacrificed some things that she'd wanted, and she endured various other "negatives." So she'd sworn to her unconscious self that she was never doing that again—and *voilà*, she had no "one special" man in her life.

When we started to look, it was also clear that the experiences she desired to share with a man were already present. She was generating plenty of sexual energy—except that it was directed into and came from her work. When she walked me through a house that she designed, my response was, "My God, this is like a sexual encounter." In addition to the layout, which was filled with male- and female-genital symbolism, she moved through the house in an incredibly sultry way.

I said, "Look at the way you lean against that table and how you hold yourself as you move up the stairs—you're being seductive with all of your male clients, I bet."

Up until that point, she'd been totally unaware of this and thought that she was frustrated, unable to find someone with whom she could share her sexuality. She'd allowed herself the illusion that she was missing something, but everything was indeed manifesting—just according to her values, not cultural expectation or personal fantasy.

When she saw what she was doing, she admitted, "You're right! I now realize that when I complain about not having a man, it's just a response to what I think I'm *supposed* to want, not to what I really love. I actually don't want a man right now, mainly because of the negative associations that I have between them and my business. Guys threaten my real values. I don't want to be dependent; I want my own money to do whatever I want, when I want. And I crave the spotlight and refuse to live in somebody's shadow."

Her current set of priorities, including her desire for independence from powerful and controlling males, emerged from her perceptions or misperceptions of her relationships. I then applied The Demartini Method to her emotionally charged history, helped her feel gratitude and love for it, and broadened her options for manifesting her soul mate.

She realized that she was already manifesting guys in her life, but they were clients. She could be paid for her work, receive acknowledgment, and act sensuously in front of them, and still have control. At that point, she had a choice: shift her goals (which she could do in the way I explained in an earlier chapter), or honor her existing hierarchy. Either way, she could continue to share her life with her "soul mate," whether in the form she was currently experiencing or in a new way—one or many.

It may seem strange to include an example like this in a chapter on soul mates. You might imagine that I "should" only be telling you how to secure someone in your life instead of how you might choose another path altogether.

There's the crux of it, however, and I hope that it's starting to sink in: It doesn't matter whether you're unattached or with another person—perceiving yourself as unlucky in love or head over heels—**your soul mate is already with you, manifesting as a single form or many that you may or may not be recognizing.**

How to Be Sure You'll Experience Love

In the mythical book of love, you'll find another core tenet alongside *Be yourself,* which is *Love yourself first.* Again, this may sound as though you should be thinking, *Oh, I need to build up my self-worth so that I appear confident to others, which will make me attractive; and therefore my soul mate will show up and want to be with me.*

Although you're probably more appealing to others when you're self-confident, that's not how I mean *Love yourself* at all. For you to experience the affection that someone else has for you, "warts and all," you'd be wise to cherish *yourself* fully. This means choosing to see yourself in 360 degrees, with your unique expression of every character trait. It also means realizing that you encompass a truly perfect, complementary collection. When you embrace this, your dark and light, your positive and negative—in sum, your supposed duality, of which the so-called parts are actually indistinguishable—then you're ready to experience unity.

Finding this with another person involves embracing who each of you is and what each of you brings to the relationship: two distinct perceptions and ways of thinking and feeling about the world. This is what I call the *love dance,* where both partners learn to embrace all parts of themselves and of one another. Think of The Demartini Method that you learned and used as Arthur Murray–style "footprints," showing you where to step so that you dance as gracefully as possible.

You're the Moon and the Sun

Let's switch gears for a moment and travel back several thousand years. Have you heard the Egyptian legend of Isis and Osiris? It's interesting to explore because it touches on this theme of "parts," and it provides insight into our modern marriage ceremony.

Here's the legend in a nutshell: Osiris and Isis were deities of the Nile Delta, children of Geb (Earth) and Nut (Sky).

They ruled Egypt together as husband and wife, and they were constantly on guard against their brother, Set, who was jealous of them.

They were smart to be nervous, because the minute that Set got the opportunity, he had Osiris murdered; specifically, the god was drowned in the Nile in a golden coffin. Weeping, Isis went in search of her brother-husband, hoping to resurrect him. Although she did find him, Set devised another way to keep Osiris from coming back: He had his brother chopped into 14 pieces and scattered across Egypt. He knew that Isis couldn't perform her ritual without finding all the parts of her beloved. [Nice metaphor, right? You can't unite with your loved one until you discover all of their aspects and honor them.]

So Isis went on a quest to find every piece. Each time she recovered some part of Osiris, she set up a shrine, and then carried it with her. Eventually, she found all but the phallus and resurrected Osiris. [I wouldn't put much emphasis on the missing bit; I can't quite see how it's relevant here, except that, miraculously, Isis conceived her son, Horus, without it. Perhaps we can say that she was divinely fertile and creative with or without a penis in her life, not unlike the interior designer I told you about earlier.]

This legend has been around for ages, dating to before recorded history. And Isis had an incredibly long run as the principal feminine deity. Her mythology influenced many other cults and religions, including Christianity. The oldest church in Paris (Par-Isis, "the grove of Isis") is Saint-Germain-des-Prés, which was built over a former temple of Isis, and a black statue of her was worshipped there as a Virgin Mary until 1514.

Isis represents the female aspect of the divine, and she has morphed into many goddesses and symbols through time. She's strong and integrated. Take note of these words of power attributed to her in *The Metamorphoses* (taken from *The Transformation of Lucius, Otherwise Known as the Golden Ass*, by Lucius Apuleius):

> I am Nature, the universal Mother, mistress of all the elements, primordial child of time, sovereign of all things spiritual, queen of the dead, queen also of the immortals, the single manifestation of all gods and goddesses that are. My nod governs the shining heights of Heaven, the wholesome sea-breezes, the lamentable silences of the world below. Though I am worshipped in many aspects, known by countless names, and propitiated with all manner of different rites, yet the whole round earth venerates me.

Add in astronomy, and the legend gets even more fascinating. My late wife and I wrote a detailed account of this in our 1993 book, *The Sacred Journey of Soul Mates*. For purposes of this chapter, I'm going to give you an overview so that you can get a sense of how this works.

Remember, Isis was the daughter of Earth and Sky, and people made her their moon goddess, the archetypal female: cool, white, moist, receptive, and reflective. The sun, not surprisingly, was associated with Osiris, the archetypal male: hot, red, fiery, active, and projective.

If you consider the 28 phases of the moon, you can translate some of astronomy into the love dance between the moon goddess and her cohort, the sun god.

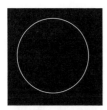

Figure 4. **Phases 1–3, New Moon:** From Earth, we don't see the moon, except perhaps an outline of it against the dark sky.

Figure 5. **Phases 4–7, Waxing Crescent:** The moon is less than half illuminated as we see it.

Figure 6. **Phases 8–10, First Quarter:** Now we see half the moon.

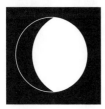

Figure 7. **Phases 11–14, Waxing Gibbous:** More than half the moon is revealed to us.

Figure 8. **Phase 15, Full Moon:** Now that the moon has come into full illumination, it begins its waning cycle: it will wane to a crescent; move into the last quarter (half revealed again); decrease to gibbous; and then go to the first phase again, the new moon. The entire cycle takes approximately 28 days.

Since ancient times (before the idea of solar calendars), people have examined the movement of the moon across the background of fixed stars and made calendars based on this study. The month started with one new moon and ended with the next. Since this orb moves across the fixed stars in a time period of 27 or 28 days (a sidereal month, which is actually 27.321661 days), its zodiacal path in the sky was divided into 27 or 28 parts; and each of these lunar asterisms was named after a prominent star in it, each conceived of as a wife to moon.

During this time (a month according to the ancient calendars), Earth shifts in its orbit around the sun, and the period between new moons is 29 or 30 days (a synodic month, which is 29.530589 days on average). This results in the asterism in the background of the full moon advancing by two or three steps each time. So months were named after the background constellation on the full-moon night, and these are still the labels we use, even though they're now defined in terms of the position of the sun against the fixed stars (a sidereal year of 365.256363 days).

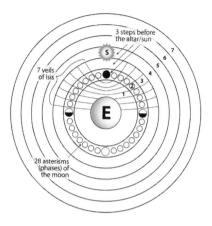

Figure 9.

Left	Right
Male Side	Female Side
Sun = Osiris	Moon = Isis
Seven Groomsmen	Seven Bridesmaids

Three steps to the altar (realm 4, the sun) from the earth (realm 1)

The legend states that when the moon is dark, Isis is closer to Osiris, facing him and turning her back on the earth. To Osiris, she's completely unveiled.

As the moon goes through its first seven phases, Isis becomes less and less "seen" by Osiris. These stages are therefore also called the seven veils of Isis. For a time, she's hidden from her husband-brother, veiling herself and returning to her offspring, Horus, the earthly king. With the waning of the moon, Isis unveils herself (the seven asterisms of the last quarter) and becomes naked before her lover. With the new moon, Isis turns her back on the terrestrial world and embraces the immortal lifegiver, Osiris, the sun.

Today, we have a ceremony symbolizing this, even if we don't acknowledge the ritual's basis in astronomical theology while we're doing it. It's our Western marriage ceremony, where the woman removes her bridal veil to become one with the man. The bridesmaids represent phases of the moon, as do the groomsmen. Anything going up toward the sun and to the left symbolizes the masculine; what goes down and to the right represents the feminine—and at the wedding, everyone associated with the groom is on the left, and the bride is on the right.

A couple exchanges golden rings, which signify the sun; and in Christianity, "Son" symbolism is identified as the love of God the Father. The bride remains hidden until she steps up and becomes one with her betrothed when their marriage has been sanctified. Then the groom lifts her veil and seals their union with a kiss.

The ritual mimes the moon facing the sun, turning its back on mortality and becoming eternal through union with it, transcending the earthly plane with its mundane perceptions and transient emotions into the infinite, which is love.

It's not just about eating cake, dancing till dawn, and making a promise of forever. It's about eternal, unflinching, unconditional love, being seen in your fullness, and embracing one another in moments of complete revelation.

Lifting the Veil for Good

In our culture, however, marriage doesn't automatically lead to full disclosure. More often than not, even though a couple has both literally and figuratively seen one another naked, this doesn't mean that the fullness of the relationship has been realized. This can only happen when both people are willing to see and embrace one another without the emotional extremes of infatuation or resentment. People who've "found" their soul mates are the ones who are momentarily not controlled or conditioned by their oppositional emotions.

This doesn't mean that you no longer feel or are subject to the fears, guilt, elations, and depressions of everyday life. It does mean that you can briefly see through the veil to the real person and embrace him or her in whole in a moment of gratitude and true unconditional love. Thus, the _soul_ becomes a **Spirit Of Unconditional Love.**

You won't experience a profound connection as long as you project your values (and, therefore, conditions) onto people, judge them as positive or negative, and refuse to open your heart. Once you've opened yourself to all that is, as it is, you're ready for your soul mate.

If you persist in keeping yourself veiled, you won't move on to the next phase. Instead, if you choose to reveal your true power in all areas of your life, you increase the probability of meeting someone who can experience this with you. When you discover your soul mate in yourself, you can recognize it in the world, too.

Actions to Create More Fulfilling Relationships

— **Describe your imagined soul mate in great detail.**
Write down your thoughts in your notebook, putting each character trait on a separate line. When you've finished with the list, observe where and in whom it already shows up in your life. Be sure to include both positive and negative

complementary traits; otherwise, you're hoping and searching for a one-sided fantasy.

— Use The Demartini Method with people from each sign of the zodiac. People who are seeking soul mates often turn to astrology for help. It's an entertaining tool, but it's frequently misdirected. Instead of trying to recognize your partner by his or her birth date *(Let's see . . . is it Harry from the office or that guy I bumped into at the deli? What does Zelda the zodiac queen have to say . . . ?),* use astrology to help you integrate yourself.

As you know, each body comes into this world under a star sign determined by the date of birth, which provides a list of probable characteristics for that person to contend with during life. In other words, out of a possible 4,600 traits (believe me, there are that many—I counted), each star sign emphasizes a series of positive and negative attributes that you'll tend to admire or despise. Keep in mind, however, that you still have all the other signs' qualities, too; it's just that they don't trigger a strong reaction.

So here's a project for you: Choose 12 different people from the different star signs and apply The Demartini Method with each of them as the subject. This is a powerful integration exercise that can catapult you into new levels of understanding about yourself and others.

I believe that the more integrated you are, the less any of the star signs appears to rule or influence you. In your lifetime, you'll be challenged to master them—not just your own, but the whole dozen, which will come to you in the form of other people whom you'll resent or with whom you'll become infatuated.

The more you're able to see and embrace all the positive and negative aspects of the star signs (which are simply the possible good and bad traits that you may have labeled within yourself) the less influence the zodiac will have upon you, the more freedom you'll have from the destiny of the heavens, and the more you'll get to govern those stars. Astrology appears to manipulate you only to the degree that you're not yet integrated and empowered.

How do you manifest or attract a loved one, a personification of your soul mate? Integrate yourself—know, be, and love yourself!

Words of Power

I encompass all things, and so does everyone else.

My soul mate is around me 24 hours
a day, 7 days a week.

If two people are exactly the same, one
of them is not necessary.

I let others see me in my fullness so
that I may be loved.

I open myself to all that is, as it is.

I cherish all my traits, and I use them wisely.

CHAPTER EIGHT

Let's Get It On . . . and Get Over It

Why do we feel lust when we fall in love?
Because dopamine, the liquor of romance, can stimulate
the release of testosterone, the hormone of sexual desire.
— From Dr. Helen Fisher's *Why We Love:*
The Nature and Chemistry of Romantic Love

Notice of Mature Subject Matter:

This chapter addresses the topic of human
sexuality and has more explicit language and more
graphic content than the rest of this book.

Sex: There's the act itself, and it also refers to your ana-
tomy (the genitalia), as well as the genders, male and
female, plus certain characteristics called "masculine" and
"feminine." Defining sex stumped a President of the United
States, while pursuing it has started and even stopped wars.
It gets people steamed up, hot under the collar, and hot for
one another every day. But is this all about chemistry and
hormones, or something deeper and more mystical—or
both? Can you really experience desire, connection, and
intimacy with someone for the long term, or are feelings of
burnout inevitable? Is there such a thing as a relationship
with true fidelity, or is everyone bound to be unfaithful
sooner or later?

Sex, sex, sex. That little word packs a wallop, doesn't it?

It certainly elicits more laughter in my seminar programs than anything else. And it appears that this comedy often stems from some form of repressed and hidden tragedy. Countless issues and illusions surround the subject. Entire books—hundreds of them—have been written about it. What can I possibly say that you can't find anywhere else? Plenty.

If you're looking for "101 Ways to Please a Man," or "Secrets for Bringing a Woman to Orgasm in Under Five Minutes," forget it. (Just for the record, I'll state that I think most men don't require 101 ways, and most women find attempts to break the sound barrier in bed to be a turnoff.) This chapter isn't about technique, but if you're interested in getting a grip on the dynamics of sex in any relationship, then read on.

We'll be examining the influence of gender and values on sexual fulfillment, attraction, and fidelity, as well as their role in sexual expression and repression, both personally and culturally. In other words, we're exploring why and when people have great sex, why and how they "stray" from so-called committed relationships, and what happens when individuals deny their own feelings.

The Chemistry of Attraction and Attachment

What's really going on when you're attracted to someone? We've already touched on this in an earlier chapter, when I wrote about the infatuation phase. Remember, this is when you see only one side of a person: the positive traits, the potential for a happily ever after. You don't even notice that her feet stink or that he scratches his butt. No, she's Cinderella and he's Prince Charming—for now.

Your body chemistry only heightens the whole lopsided process, giving you regular doses of dopamine (a hormone that mimics the effects of cocaine), resulting in phenomena such as energy boosts, appetite suppression, heart palpitations, accelerated breathing, hyperactivity, and insomnia. Romantics say, "I love him/her so much that I can't eat, sleep, or think straight." That's the dope talking. And dopamine triggers testosterone, which means sex drive goes up, and soon enough, you're making love like bunnies.

There's no doubt that sex drive is partly chemical and hormonal, but it's also psychological and energetic. As I mentioned earlier in the book, partners in a relationship become more susceptible to outside interests when they stop honoring one another's values. It's as if a periscope goes up, out of the relationship, to scan the horizon. And males, because of their naturally higher levels of testosterone, scope things out more often than women.

This isn't to say that men are significantly more likely to stray; I think it may actually be nearly even-steven (or even-stephanie). It's just that guys probably consider their options more often. Statistics on the rates of infidelity are suspect because there's no way to gauge the honesty of survey respondents. Some people might deny activity they're ashamed of or brag about something that never happened. Yet here's something to consider: The Associated Press reported in the late 1990s that 22 percent of men and 14 percent of women admitted to having sexual relations outside their marriage sometime in their past, 70 percent of married women and 54 percent of married men didn't know about their spouse's extramarital activity, and 17 percent of divorces in the United States are caused by so-called cheating.

Interestingly enough, a man's testosterone levels go up or down, inversely proportionate with the attachment he feels in his relationship. In other words, the more attached he feels to his partner or family, the lower his testosterone levels. Right after orgasm, a man experiences a surge of vasopressin, which is thought to depress the hormone. Also, a new father's testosterone declines immediately when his child is born. In fact, it drops when he simply holds a baby, just from having parental, caretaking feelings.

Does this mean that the more attached a man is to his partner and family, the lower his testosterone levels are and, therefore, the lower his sex drive is, so he's less likely to put up his periscope? Bingo! And what creates this bond? The more he feels his values are being honored and fulfilled in the relationship, the less he feels the need to look elsewhere; both his psychology and his chemistry support this.

What creates a similar effect in women? Having her own ideals respected, of course, plus sexual fulfillment (specifically orgasm) and nursing a child, both of which trigger release of a hormone called oxytocin, the female counterpart to vasopressin.

But don't confuse attachment and its hormones with some kind of magic bullet for fidelity. Where polyamory (loving more than one) isn't restricted by cultural barriers, or in couples who choose not to comply with cultural norms, it's more freely expressed. Although "open" relationships have their own challenges, they're not inherently "worse" (or "better") than "closed" ones. Human connections can take myriad forms, all of which are valid and potentially viable.

Since many of this book's readers will, I assume, be interested in what creates monogamy, and since this often proves to be a highly challenging aspect of marriage, it's definitely worth taking some time to understand what influences people to conform with this expectation or not.

Let me just state it plainly: No one will remain sexually "faithful" unless it fits in with his or her own value hierarchy. In other words, **there's no such thing as being true to this woman or that man . . . only to one's own values.** Because all people have a complementary set of opposite traits or personas, you'll find that everyone will be more trustworthy when it comes to their higher values and less so about their lower priorities. Realize that the experience of betrayal can be half of every partnership, because people live according to their ideals, not yours.

So if such values as *monogamous marriage* and *relationship stability* are high on the list, then sexual fidelity may result. If *family* ranks above *a variety of sexual partners* and your mate is unwilling to nurture children while you have sex with other people, then you'll do your best to honor the higher value—but you might not always follow through. It's also possible that you might choose to pursue both interests and not tell your spouse. It's a recipe for so-called dishonesty and affairs when a person is being true to his or her own goals but presenting a facade to preserve a partner's fantasy.

If you'd rather not play the game of propping up one another's illusions and then getting "disappointed, devastated, or dumped," and you'd prefer to get to the heart of love in your relationship, then find out what's important to the other person and don't try to project your ideals onto him or her. You're wise to pay attention both to what someone says and what he or she does. When you're just getting to know someone, it's not a good idea to overwhelm him or her with your own fantasies about relationships, but instead to really understand and honor that individual.

How do you do this? First and foremost, make it advantageous for the other person to be honest with you, *because that's the only circumstance under which someone will do so.* In other words, practice hearing someone else's truth without expressing your judgments about whether it's "good" or "bad" (that is, whether it matches or mismatches your own values) and without trying to give punishments or rewards for specific values. You can do this by using The Demartini Method to defuse whatever "charges" you have on this person, whether positive or negative.

Please understand that people will only be up-front when they perceive more advantages in doing so than disadvantages, according to their values, and they'll be deceitful when they believe it's in their best interest. People are forthright and misleading in different settings, although most will imagine themselves as only one (honest) and deny their other attribute.

Completing The Demartini Method will also help you wake up to your own disowned parts so that you're able to proceed with balance instead of being driven by extremes. Consider the dynamics of the "overdog" and underdog, which I first described in an earlier chapter. In couples, those who perceive themselves with the least overall power in the seven areas of life seek more monogamy (apparent constraint); those who see themselves as having the most strength seek more polygamy (apparent freedom). Generally, the extreme monogamist feels compelled to marry and "settle down," while the ardent polygamist is driven to remain single and "run free."

Extremely powerful polygamists attract others who exhibit their disowned parts—extremely powerless monogamists—to neutralize their expressed qualities and to teach the balance of love, and vice versa.

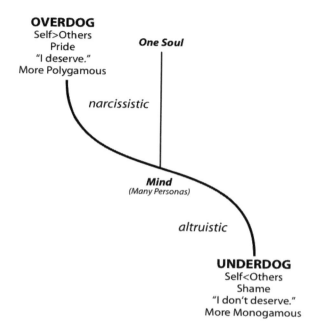

Figure 10. Overdogs see themselves as greater than others, and seek more polygamous relationships; underdogs see themselves as less than others and seek more monogamous partnerships.

When you allow this imbalance to persist in your relationships, you're likely to start playing familiar roles, such as parent and child or controller and controlled. Although this dynamic will occur to some degree in any relationship, the more equal the two people feel, the narrower the oscillation will seem—in other words, you moderate the interplay of power instead of having one person at each extreme. The greater the difference, however, the more it dampens sexual desire. "I married my mother (or father)" is the complaint of someone who's become an extreme underdog in some domain and whose partner has become the parent. "Smothering" and "controlling" don't usually foster sexual closeness.

Couples who perceive an equality of overall powers maintain a wise balance of monogamous (one) and polygamous (many) thoughts and actions and keep each other in check. This creates a more stable bond that has wholeness and wellness. Remember, when you're dating the many, you seek the one; and when you're with the one, you're wondering about the many. This law rules all relationships.

— **If you imagine yourself to be the overdog in a relationship, look carefully to see where your so-called underdog partner has unacknowledged power,** and possibly help him or her become awakened to it. Use The Demartini Method with this person as the subject so that you can realize the inherent balance that already exists. In the meantime, consider not buying into any pressure of marriage unless your heart, intuition, and reason all say that this is the person and it's time. Trying to appease someone else, evade feeling alone, or avoid the appearance of a supposedly undesirable trait— such as *distant, unavailable,* or *someone with "commitment issues"*—is to play out that same underdog side yourself.

— **If you're an acknowledged underdog in a relationship, find ways to help yourself wake up to your own power.** Use The Demartini Method with your overdog partner as the subject so that you can loosen your grip and learn to embrace your own wholeness instead. When you awaken to your already-present (yet currently hidden) power, your urgency for marriage relaxes, which magnetically draws the other person to you even more. Few if any people truly desire the desperate and disempowered as mates.

— **Seek to acknowledge and unfold your power in all seven areas:** spiritual, mental, vocational, financial, familial social, and physical. When you do this, you'll find that your "stock" goes up in the realm of relationships. The more you have to offer, the more options you have. When you can see the opportunities, you stop feeling "trapped" or "compelled." You experience your ability to choose and to participate fully in the creation of your life and relationships.

After you've completed The Demartini Method with your partner, go back to the two chapters on values and do the exercises there, too. Try to keep your head out of the hormonal cloud—or at least come up for air often enough that you can see more clearly. Delay promises of "forever," "always," and "my one and only" until the infatuation phase has run its course. And if someone would love to have a different kind of connection than the one he or she has with you, then acknowledge this both to yourself and to that person. Realize that maybe there's just not a fit between the two of you at this time. Don't see this as a "failed" relationship or beat yourself (or someone else) up just because you'd love different things right now.

Boredom, Baggage, and Breaking Down the Fantasies

At the beginning of a relationship, chemistry can be challenging because it tends to foster fantasies and nurture misperceptions; and as time goes on, it can present new challenges. *Where did that fire go? Why don't we feel so attracted* to each other anymore? Is this all there is? What happened to all the hot sex? You may start measuring the state of your sexual connection against an illusion created by the infatuation you experienced, either in this relationship or another one. The dopamine may have stopped flowing, but the rosy picture it created still colors your thoughts and feelings.

For example, one gentleman attended *The Breakthrough Experience* because, he said, "My marriage is boring. It's just not alive!"

I asked, "In relationship to what? What are you comparing it to?"

He told me about something that had happened more than ten years before, when he'd gone to an upscale resort to meet a few of his buddies. As he arrived, a woman from London was checking in at the same time. Since he'd gotten to the hotel before his friends, he gave her his full attention. There she was, wearing a crop top and short white pants, looking most appealing. He asked, "Why don't we meet over at the pool bar in 30 minutes?"

They met and had a few drinks, and then went up to his room to spend the next few days in bed, getting it on, resting and eating only when they had to. There was a Jacuzzi in the suite and great room service, which was all they needed. Basically, they had sex for three days straight. He didn't answer the phone or call his girlfriend in the United States. He didn't even talk to his buddies who were there and wondering where the hell he was, although they called his room continually to find out what was wrong with him.

He and the woman had this passionate experience, and then she went back to London. They both acknowledged that it was too great a distance for the connection to go anywhere, and he wanted to go back to his relationship anyway.

Later, he broke up with his girlfriend, and a few years went by before he met and married his wife. By the time he arrived at my seminar, he was comparing his three-year-old marriage to a weekend "sexcapade" that had occurred more than a decade ago—which was an experience no woman could endure for more than three days! His fantasy and infatuation were causing a low-grade "blahness" in his current union and a sense of lack of fulfillment in the rest of his life.

He was comparing everything else to this exaggerated experience, and until he broke that mirage, it would continue to run his life. So I helped him come up with the drawbacks of being with the British woman. I asked him to list the negative things about being with her, and he exclaimed, "Oh, man, there were none!"

I replied, "Well, look again! There were. What negatives did you experience? What were the pains of those three days?"

He still said that he couldn't see any, and he kept repeating that until he finally admitted, "Well, okay, I did feel some guilt because I didn't call my girlfriend."

"Was that gnawing on you? That's fine. What else?"

"I did feel some regret because my buddies were there, and they expected to work out and have some fun together. Part of their cost included my share of things, and I didn't participate, so they were a bit angry with me. I alienated my friends."

"What else? What about her? What were the drawbacks of her, specifically?"

He insisted, "Man, I don't know."

I pressed him: "Look again, because every human being has traits that you admire and despise. Don't ever think that you're going to get more admiration than revulsion, even physically."

"Well, okay. She did have shorter legs than I like, and her hair was kind of thin, until it was washed. Her voice was kind of whiny."

"What else?"

"Her thighs were a little heavy, thicker than I usually go for."

"What else?"

"She wasn't really ambitious, and she wasn't too bright. She had a lot of emotional baggage from her past relationships."

"What else?"

"Yeah . . . now that I think about it, there *were* some drawbacks."

I pointed out, "You were unwilling to see them during moments of passion and idolizing her because you were blinded. You see, infatuation and resentment can't see, but true love observes the whole. It notices both positive and negative elements equally. I'll repeat that because it's so important: **Infatuation is blind to the negatives, and resentment can't see the positives. True love is whole and witnesses both sides equally.**"

We continued talking until he could take this vacation lover off her pedestal. As he started moving that fantasy down in his estimation, his wife came back up. He began to appreciate her more as he unraveled the previous infatuation and saw that there was no way his wife could compete with a three-day experience. Any woman can be 100 percent sex kitten for such a short period of time, but maintaining it for much longer is another story. He could see how he'd bought into unrealistic expectations. As we broke this delusion and added pain to what had been seen as only pleasure, he began to wake up to the benefits of his current marital experience.

This is a story where a guy went on vacation and came home with more than he'd taken with him. *Baggage is any imbalanced perspective.* Everyone brings this into relationships—and it's the purpose and nature of connecting with another person to help you set down that load.

Of course, you do have a choice: You can either let it go or continue to carry it with you. When you start thinking, *All guys are this* or *All girls are that,* you carry those misperceptions into the next union, and the next, and they get reinforced by your inability or unwillingness to see anything else. You become something of an automaton programmed to react when certain things happen again, which they inevitably will, because all humans have all traits.

Can you see that you have baggage? So does everyone else with whom you interact, although you may not have illusions about the same things. A man may buy his lover roses, for example, expecting her to gush over the romantic gesture. Instead, he gets an explosion because the last guy did so only because he'd had an affair! That guy had never got her anything until he had a fling with her best friend, and then he came home with a big bouquet, thinking that would solve it. So she carries that bit of baggage: Anyone who shows up with roses is an insensitive bastard!

Deciding to Heal

One fellow attended my seminar with his wife, and he complained, "I don't know what's wrong with her. As soon as she comes to orgasm, she just curls up in a fetal position and starts crying! I ask her, 'Am I hurting you?' She says, 'No, no,' and keeps sobbing. She doesn't ever want to have sex anymore, and I'm not sure I do, either, if that's how it's going to be."

The man was deeply concerned for his wife, and demoralized. He couldn't see how to change things, and his spouse was too frightened to explain to him what was really going on with her. (Incidentally, just as there's always balance in the world, it also exists in my seminars. At this same event was a woman who was a professional pole dancer. It was the perfect example: A public sexual excessor and a private sexual repressor were sitting across from one another.)

In time, I discovered that the man's wife had had an incestuous relationship with her brother, and she'd never gotten past her confusion over sexual guilt, pain, and pleasure. She'd kept the baggage and hadn't yet come to grips with the dynamics that had given rise to the situation. As a result, anytime she had sex, especially from behind, she brought up all that she'd stored away from her past experience and shut down in a fetal position. She didn't know how to sort out her perceptions, and her husband felt trapped in a relationship with someone who brought her despair to their sex life. They were "stuck."

We used The Demartini Method to deal with the incest issue and get past it. After that, she didn't have the same reaction to sex with her husband—no more fetal position, crying, or otherwise reexperiencing her past in the present. I helped the man see what was driving her reactions and understand the logic in her response. Another key moment for him was realizing that he always has a choice about the kind of relationship he wants to create.

Claiming Your Power to Choose

Everyone has a different set of baggage, and a couple's unique combination creates its own dynamic—and each of us can decide whether we want to continue in that situation or not. No one has to be in any partnership forever. You can say, "Okay, I've learned my lesson from that, and I'd rather acquire different wisdom now. This isn't where I want to stay."

You have a right to move on. If a particular connection isn't what you'd love to have in your life and your partner isn't interested in getting past his or her own stuff, you can decide to go—and deal with a new set of baggage as you grow in a different direction. (As for the couple in this story, so far as I know, they're still together. We were able to dissolve their sexuality issue, which wasn't that difficult to do.)

Your past issues will weigh heavily on you at times, someone else's will trouble them at others, and at still other times you'll both be dragged down together. Sometimes you need a moving van, there's so much baggage! Frankly, I don't know of a more effective tool for unloading and unpacking it than The Demartini Method.

Sexual Energy and the "Deviancy" Dynamic

In the story I just told you, I touched on the need to understand the dynamics that lead to such situations as incest. Those sexual experiences we call "deviant" or "unnatural" might be more accurately labeled "expressed repressions," as they're the rather natural result of suppressed sexuality. By "natural," I mean predictable according to the laws of human interaction.

Culturally, it's forbidden to have sex with your immediate family (incest); it's also taboo to force someone to have sex with you (rape). Both are considered violent and harmful to the "victim." Before you get too disturbed, let me explain why I put the word *victim* in quotes. Under the law, victims are clearly defined, and that makes sense. But we're not in a courtroom here; we're talking about psychology, and you're wise to admit that victimhood is more a state of mind than a fact of history. No doubt you're acquainted with people who've surrendered to their past and allowed it to define them (just tune in to Jerry Springer's show to see some in action), just as you know individuals who've chosen to view their history as experiences from which they can respond with strength and increased wisdom. So I'm inclined to say that there are no victims, just illusions of victimhood.

These misperceptions can perpetuate an experience. For example, when a woman becomes highly angry with men, the emotional charge sucks in guys who connect with that energy. The view her as a sex object, a plaything, instead of a whole person; and men who have repressed (or expressed) desire for no-strings, no-intimacy sex get hooked. In other words, something in them responds when a woman's inner cry is "Screw you!" That reply is, "Okay, baby! Let's go!"

I'm not arguing that a woman's state of mind creates callousness or, in the extreme, violence. Those traits already exist in males, and in females, too, for that matter. I'm saying that her baggage can get jumbled up with someone else's and re-create the situation that she most wants to avoid.

Not that long ago, I was conducting a seminar when a woman in her 20s walked across the room to go to the bathroom. As she went by, every guy turned his head to watch her leave. Their tongues were practically hanging out as they mentally grabbed her ass and had their way with her right there in the conference room; even some of the women started to squirm in their seats as she got near them. What was going on? This was a nice-looking person, but not an unusually beautiful or sexy one. Yet the whole room was salivating over her, noticeably unnerved by some palpable sexual energy.

When she came back, I stopped my lecture and said to the group, "This young woman has either been raped or incested, and that's the energy that's attracting everyone."

I turned to her and asked, "Which one is it?"

"Well, actually, both," she told us.

"Mmm-hmm. You have the classic energy. Do you keep attracting men who want you purely for sex?"

She said, "That's my whole life."

So we used The Demartini Method to neutralize her past and help her balance her own perspective on what had happened to her, and the lust energy lifted. For the first time, people in the room noticed how beautiful her eyes were. The attention had moved off her back door and onto the windows of her soul.

Because "victims" have the power to change their sexual energy and, therefore, the experiences they attract, does this mean that they're to blame for what's happened "to" them? No, we're all participants in a larger dynamic. **What the collective society represses, selective society expresses.** A so-called victim is said to have been harmed by rape or incest, and so these actions are deemed despicable and called crimes.

By disowning parts of our sexual selves and projecting them onto people we call criminals, we're powering the cycle. Without repression, there would be no need for a "sexual predator" to express it. The entire society contributes to the actions of its so-called criminals, and we'd be wise to recognize it and start dealing with our own shadows.

Similarly, within the family unit, parental repressions can get expressed by the children; when a couple has no offspring, the balance of traits gets maintained between the two of them (unless there's an affair). The more intensely you express your owned, lawful, licit, pure, faithful, chaste, abstinent, prudish, celibate, non-adultering persona, the more likely your mate is to show extremes of your disowned, unlawful, illicit, impure, unfaithful, promiscuous, licentious, adultering persona.

When there are children in the family, there are simply more people to balance the owned/disowned traits—but the equilibrium will be preserved. When parents attempt to become the utmost idealized versions of themselves as role models for their kids, they can trigger in their children the very traits they're trying to deny in themselves.

Fear and guilt promote extremes of owned and disowned personas, and a deficiency or excess of sexuality is a result of underlying fear and guilt. How, then, can you create a relationship, a family, a community, and a society with a balanced sexual energy, one that's not driven by these emotions?

Empower ("own") all seven areas: spiritual, mental, vocational, financial, familial, social, and physical. The Demartini Method, again, can provide you with opportunities to gain wisdom and insights about your owned and disowned parts without rashly acting them out, either aggrandizing or denigrating them. You can find ways to bring the shadow to light, to safely express your "darkness" so that no one else has to do it for you.

Common sense dictates that your wise soul won't always "conquer" your body's sexual passions, which cling to you as long as you inhabit your physical self. It's wisest not to condemn these desires but to temper them instead. The point of moderation, in any case, would be determined by the comparison of the average libido or needs of the two individuals in question. Someone desiring sex three times a day would probably be labeled an "addict" by someone who wants it only once a week; the once-a-weeker might be called "repressed." Relative deficiencies or excesses can create the feelings and perceptions of stunted or stagnated personal growth.

If sex is running your life one way or the other—whether you must avoid it or have to have it, disgust or lust—you're out of balance. Moderation and transformation is the wisest and truest form of sublimation, while extreme repression is the "falsest." Since sexuality, like all energy, is conserved through time and space, it never dissipates; it just changes form. Frustration occurs when people perceive extremes. It's only with a loving and open heart that these two opposed viewpoints return to harmony—which is just one of the many reasons for using The Demartini Method.

When you make love with an open heart, it can lead to a mystical moment. When you balance perceptions between yourself and your mate, and when gratitude and love arise, sexual fulfillment occurs. This happens when you're your true being, when perfect poise has been brought into your awareness, and appreciation and love for what is, as it is, occurs. This is where the eyes and hearts of the lovers meet.

Achieving Sexual Fulfillment

Plenty of detours mark the road to this kind of contentment. Potholes abound, and cumbersome baggage can make the journey awkward and difficult. Yet if those mystical moments—love, grace, and appreciation in the midst of intimacy—are important to you, there's much you can do to help make the trip go more smoothly. In the following pages, I've identified ten keys to sexual fulfillment. Obviously, this isn't about inventive tongue techniques or gymnastic positions. It's about honoring your partner and his or her values and connecting in such a way that reflexive lust doesn't become the standard by which you judge every other sexual encounter.

10 Keys to Sexual Fulfillment

1.   **Enter into sexual relations only when you can do so with a clear head, heart, and mind.** Here's a thought: What if people who were going to engage in sex with one another took the time to read and sign a "Safety-First Guarantee"? Okay, I'm joking a little, but on another level, I'm also serious.

Safety-First Guarantee for Women

This certifies that I, the undersigned female about to enjoy sexual intercourse with _____, am above the lawful age of consent, am in my right mind, and am not under the influence of any drug or narcotic. Neither does this person have to use any force, threats, or promises to influence me.

I am in no fear of my new sexual partner whatsoever and don't expect or want to marry this person. I'm not asleep or drunk and am entering into this relation with this person because I love it and want it as much as they do. If I receive the satisfaction I expect, I'm very willing to play an early return engagement.

Furthermore, I agree never to appear as a witness against this person or to prosecute under the Man/Woman Slave Act or expect them to be responsible in any way if I become impregnated.

Signed before jumping into bed,

the _____ day of _____, 20_____.

By:

Address:

Phone:

Safety-First Guarantee for Men

This certifies that I, the undersigned male about to enjoy sexual intercourse with _____, am above the lawful age of consent, am in my right mind, and am not under the influence of any drug or narcotic. Neither does this person have to use any force, threats, or promises to influence me.

I am in no fear of my new sexual partner whatever and don't expect or want to marry this person. I'm not asleep or drunk and am entering into this relation with this person because I love it and want it as much as they do. If I receive the satisfaction I expect, I'm very willing to play an early return engagement.

Furthermore, I agree never to appear as a witness against this person or to prosecute under the Man/Woman Slave Act or expect to have any rights to a child if my partner becomes impregnated.

Signed before jumping into bed,

the _____ day of _____, 20_____.

By:

Address:

Phone:

2. **Use The Demartini Method specifically to address your own sexuality.** *What do you dislike or disown about yourself sexually?* For example, many people don't like the way they look, and they shut down because they can't stand the idea of someone else seeing, touching, or enjoying them—all because they disapprove of their own bodies. Using The Demartini Method, you may discover that the very thing that holds you back turns your partner on.

3. **Use The Demartini Method to deal with your partner's sexuality.** Defuse anything you fear or don't like

about your partner. Write it down: *How do you express this trait? Who sees it in you in some form or fashion? What are the benefits to you? What would be the drawbacks if your partner exhibited the opposing quality? Who does the opposite at the exact time that your partner exhibits this disliked attribute?* Believe it or not, you'll find that it's all there . . . if you look.

4. **Exchange and express all your repressions.** What would you love to have in your sexual life but have been hesitant or even afraid to act out or ask for? Write down all your ideas and then share them with your partner so that he or she will *know* and won't have to guess. Wouldn't you agree that if you knew what your partner would love—especially that secret, sexy thing—you'd have a higher probability of satisfying him or her?

5. **Practice giving your partner sexual fulfillment.** I don't recommend too much tantric reserve or intentionally holding back from release in order to warehouse sexual/creative energy. A little bit is okay, but you're unwise to live your life without orgasms if you're capable of having them. Not only does it set you up for attachment issues, especially for women, but many prostate and urinary tract problems can result.

6. **Practice having your partner give you sexual fulfillment.** Be sure to let the other person know what you love. Be specific! Don't make him or her guess. Instead, anytime you're feeling aroused by something, let it be known: "Yes, yes, yes! Right there! You got it!" Express yourself clearly, either with words or other unambiguous sounds. If your partner can't understand without explicit assistance, then point, demonstrate, or help by giving more

direct verbal feedback, or do whatever it takes. Guide him or her as much as you can.

7. **Focus on honoring one another's values and unique expressions of power.** Be sure to pay serious attention to what's important to the other person, as I've outlined in previous chapters. Remember that sexual fulfillment equals values fulfillment. Encourage one another in realizing the inherent balance in the relationship. If one tends toward extreme underdog and the other toward extreme overdog, you can choose to wake up together—to realize the unique expression of power in *both* people. Again, The Demartini Method can facilitate this awakening.

8. **Maintain a balance of sex with yourself (masturbation) and with the one you love (coital intercourse).** Solitary self-expression serves social other-expression, and vice versa. Both are to be mastered. You'll satisfy and gratify yourself part of the time and your mate at other points; he or she will do the same. This helps you share what satisfies you, and assists the other person in doing so as well.

9. **Identify your partner's styles and preferences.** Some like it fast, some like it slow, some like kissing beforehand, while some don't even want to look at you. Some like masks, saying other people's names, "dirty" talk, or "clean" talk ("Thou shalt go left! Hallelujah!"). Some people like silence.

By the way, if there's language you like to use when you're masturbating, say it with your partner, and watch what happens! Share whatever words or other mood setters you use in your private sexual expression. Also realize that there will be a balance between you and your partner in your preferences. The more you desire quantity, the more the other person may desire quality. This also holds true for active initiative and passive receptivity, the same form of sex act and a different version, and so on.

10. Use visual, auditory, and kinesthetic stimuli. Put all the senses—sounds, smells, tastes, touches, and sights—into the experience, and your satisfaction and intimacy increase exponentially. Here are a couple of generalizations:

- Men more commonly enjoy visual stimuli, while women often prefer the tactile. That's why more toys are sold to females and more pictures to males. Give a man a dildo for his birthday, and he's likely to respond, "Huh?" But give him a lap dance, and he'll probably say "Wow!" Most guys like to see sex and enjoy a moving target—they love to shoot their arrows at something; most women like to feel, to be touched and caressed.

- I'm fond of saying, "Men are visual, women are kinesthetic, and they try to communicate in the auditory." Just realize the differences and do your best to give your partner what he or she would love.

Actions to Create More Fulfilling Relationships

— **Use The Demartini Method with someone you "could never" make love with.** What are your reasons? Neutralize that extreme repulsion.

— **Use The Demartini Method with someone you "would always" make love with.** What are your reasons? Neutralize that extreme attraction.

Words of Power

I recognize that people are faithful to their own values, not to one another.

I move into the heart of love by finding out what's important to the other and not projecting my ideals.

I reclaim my disowned parts so that I can move forward with balanced perceptions and affection.

Infatuation is blind to the negatives, and resentment is blind to the positives. I choose true love in order to see both sides equally.

What collective society represses, selective society expresses.

❊❊❊ ❊❊❊

CHAPTER NINE

When You Think It's Over:
Dealing With Feelings of Grief and Loss

This is the thing that in the greatest is a shining light, a pure white fire; and in the humblest is a constant radiance, a quiet perpetual gleam. When we stop running away . . . that is when even tragedy succumbs to beauty.
— Katherine Mansfield

People experience heartbreak as a predictable part of life. Few, if any, get to adulthood without having undergone what they believe to be some kind of deprivation. But certain so-called tragedies stand out as bigger and "badder," don't they? These tend to challenge our ideas about loss, gain, and transformation. Yet when we study them, they can actually bolster our confidence in the integrity and unending wholeness not only of our world, but also of the universe. In time, we can come back to the realization that apparent endings, such as death or divorce, don't actually mean that we're relinquishing anything; they're a form of transformation. Just as nothing's gained from someone else, nothing's lost, either.

No doubt you're aware that in December 2004 a tsunami hit Southeast Asia, "killing" hundreds of thousands of people. For those who watched coverage of the event on the news, the apparent devastation was quite shocking. For the ones who experienced it firsthand, the enormity of the event was nearly indescribable. Nearly "losing" your life, being "violently" separated from family members and perhaps never finding their bodies, watching people you know get carried away in a rush of water, having your belongings disappear out to sea . . . no words fully capture the apparent "disaster."

To make the assertion that nothing was lost in this event could be considered simpleminded and in poor taste. Yet there were indeed counterbalances to the sweeping "tragedy." For example, in Indonesia's hardest-hit region, the Aceh Province, political changes came quickly as a result of the disaster. The area had been in conflict for 30 years, with rebels striving for independence and tens of thousands dying on both sides of the cause. Within months of the tsunami, peace talks began in earnest. The catastrophe changed the political and psychological landscape, too, as both parties decided that there was something more important to do than fight. Whereas before, people had been dying every day in battle, the water swept away the social war and left survivors to rebuild in a semblance of public "peace." Of course, the incentives for harmony emerged as both parties faced the challenging prospects brought on by geology and nature, so ultimately the law of transformation was conserved.

You might think, *Okay, that's fine for that small area, but what about all those people who lost their homes and, more important, their friends and loved ones? How can you say that they haven't lost anything? Isn't that just positive thinking run amok?*

Well, I'd like to tell you about a woman I met near Bangkok, Thailand. Jane's husband died in the tsunami, and she almost drowned. Some acquaintances she'd been socializing with at her hotel when the giant wave hit were yanked away from her and perished in the wall of water, also. When I met her six months after the event, she was still feeling deeply saddened by her experience.

Wake Up to Love

Jane attended a Wellness Summit conference where I was a guest speaker. She approached me because I'd claimed to be able to help anyone who felt that they'd experienced loss move past their pain and return to a state of gratitude and love—in about three hours. I invited the people at my presentation to contact me and arrange to meet me so that we could test what some thought was an empty, arrogant boast.

Later that same day, I met Jane in person and used The Demartini Method to help her come to a new understanding so that she could move on with her life. I worked with her for less than the projected three hours, asking her the same questions I'll present to you at the end of this chapter:

- What exactly do you feel you've lost?

- What's the new form being displayed in your life now?

- What's the drawback of the old form?

- What's the benefit of the new form?

These are powerful questions to ask when you've been through an event that seems so devastating and shocking that it's easy to deny the continued existence of what's perceived to be gone. In times like these, it can feel "right" to leave the new forms unrecognized and unacknowledged. Yet choosing to see them, bringing these fresh manifestations to your conscious mind, isn't "positive thinking." Instead, the process helps you become both full participator in—and objective observer of—your own life.

When I returned to the conference the following day, Jane and a couple of the others shared what we'd done together. Among them was a couple whose son had "died." When some of the attendees asked those I'd worked with if they were genuinely free from their grief, they confirmed that they were.

They'd all realized that this emotion is really a form of incomplete awareness, and the only thing they'd lost was sight of the fact that these were events of transformation, not actual endings or loss. I like to call remorse, grief, sorrow, and bereavement *withdrawal symptoms* from whatever we're infatuated with or addicted to. We don't feel loss for those we truly love, for those we fully care for remain ever-present whether they're alive or so-called dead.

Each person I had the opportunity to do The Demartini Method with had restored a balanced perspective. People talk about personal tragedies as putting you off-kilter and making it so you can't see straight. Those aren't just colorful phrases; they're actually excellent descriptions of what happens when you become enthralled by something that you perceive as being hugely negative. Of course, that's also what occurs when you become infatuated with something you perceive as hugely positive: You feel sorrow when you believe that you've lost the object of your adoration. Nobody mourns the perceived loss of that which they resent—instead, they feel relieved and free. Imbalance is imbalance, and uneven perception is blinding.

Clarifying Your Vision

When Andrea attended one of my seminars, she was grieving the loss of her husband, who'd committed suicide about a year before. She told me that she was still in great pain and just couldn't seem to let go, and that she felt her sorrow kept her connected to the "best man I've ever known."

Like many people who find themselves wishing that they could revive a relationship whose time has passed, Andrea had become infatuated with an idea of who her husband had been. She had put him on a pedestal and was longing to live in the fantasy that she'd created about their marriage, pining for something she knew she could never have again: that specific man in that particular body. She claimed that he'd been so wonderful that he'd spoiled her for anyone else, and she'd spend the rest of her life mourning his passing.

When I pressed her to recall anything that wasn't positive about their marriage so that she could break her addictive fantasy, she wept and said that there was nothing in their life together that wasn't beautiful, magical, and loving. But when I asked her, gently but pointedly, why such a man would commit suicide, she started to consider what might really have been true for him—and for her. She slowly started to acknowledge that his depression was a difficult part of their lives, he'd struggled with the urge to kill himself for months, and he'd perceived himself as experiencing great pain. She even recalled that when he was having a dark day, he'd try to hurt her, too—not physically, but his attempts to distance himself emotionally from her had taken their toll.

Finally, the floodgates opened for her. She was able to see her husband, herself, and their life together with a more balanced perspective. She could remember both the apparent good and the bad, the wonderful and the terrible, the nice and the mean, the depression and elation, and so on. She was able to feel her love for this man well up and overtake the grief that had resulted from her broken fantasy, and she was able to move forward in her life—not as a stricken widow, but as a woman who'd reclaimed her gratitude and wonder for all that life had given her and would continue to provide.

I wrote in my book *The Breakthrough Experience* that between extreme particles is the center point of light, and between exaggerated emotions is the balance of love. Because of this, every tragedy and triumph holds the promise of balance; each so-called heartbreak signals the destruction of a fantasy. Indeed, it's not your heart that's breaking; it's your illusions about yourself, others, or the world. When those fantasies are destroyed, you have the freedom to see what's true—the center point of love. You realize your ability to fully experience that feeling, which is a synthesis and synchronicity of opposites.

If The Demartini Method could help someone with something so seemingly overwhelming as Jane's experience with the tsunami or Andrea's journey after her husband's suicide, you can have confidence that it will help you get through a breakup, a separation, a divorce, or even the death of a loved one. Despair and grief following a relationship's "end" are common, but they don't truly have to exist or be prolonged. You can do something about your imbalanced perspectives by using my method, and specifically the portion of it I've included at the end of this chapter. You can wake up and become adaptable to—and present with—the immediate transformation.

You Never Gain or Lose Anything Within or Around You

In case you skipped the rest of this book and came right to this chapter, let me reiterate that all of the many hundreds of human traits are conserved through time and change only in form, not just within a single individual but also throughout a dynamic family unit. This idea can seem pretty abstract, so I'll give you another concrete example.

Dean was a doctor who was driven—in his practice, in continuing his education, and in his finances. He was a stereotypically type A male with a thriving practice, enjoying camaraderie with his colleagues and married to a lovely woman with whom he had five kids. His wife, Nadia, was totally focused on their children, not ambitious in business or finance, but very concerned with providing for the family and creating a wonderful life for them. These two were quite the pair of complementary opposites.

Dean came to see me because he was starting to worry about their ability to manage it all. The couple was in the midst of what I call the *second-house syndrome,* when it suddenly hit Dean that he had a new mortgage and five kids, he was working like a dog, and his wife seemed to be more interested in his children than in him. In a situation like this, both people start feeling unappreciated, as if they're living separate lives: his focused on work, and hers on home. You can guess what happens next: Someone has a fling.

That's exactly what happened here. After four months, Nadia found out that Dean was having an affair and (after she got through her initial sense of hurt and assumed betrayal) started to look at the bottom line: "Oh, no! If we divorce, I've either got to get everything I can now and sell the house to have financial liquidity, or I've got to go to work. I have to figure something out." She didn't want her children's lives to be in turmoil, and she didn't want to be embarrassed when she couldn't fix everything for them.

She started thinking, *I can't rely on him. I've got to rely on myself.*

Nadia's values began to shift as she experienced an identity crisis, and she ended up deciding that whatever happened, she was going back to college and Dean was going to pay for it, dammit.

Out of his misunderstood guilt, Dean said, "Yes, I owe you that."

Ultimately, this couple didn't divorce. They continued to live together, but the relationship remained distant. Nadia did go back to school, and their kids naturally became more independent as they got older. Dean found that he "missed" them and wanted to hang out with them, so he made a point of being more active in their lives. He adapted his medical practice so that he could work more efficiently and spend more time at home.

Right about that time, Nadia graduated with her master's degree and decided to build a business and write a book. She became driven in her new vocation. Meanwhile, Dean started taking more and more time off to be with the kids. In five years, they'd reversed roles. She became more interested in her career, and he became more focused on the kids. The very things they'd once condemned in each other, they'd become.

In this and every family, there's a hidden order and balance, and nothing's truly missing. When one person's values shift, the whole group accommodates it. Traits take on new forms and everything gets redistributed among the rest of the immediate or extended family members. If one of the parents had left the household altogether and cut off those relationships, then everyone else would have picked up the slack: Children might have begun parenting one another, and so on. The departing adult would have experienced new forms of all the old traits that were present in the former situation, too. At times, friends or relatives outside the immediate family would act in surrogate roles to fill the void.

I've worked with individuals whose parents have died, whose children have run away from home, whose spouses have left them, and who have "lost" their best friend—people who have experienced every form of being "left" that exists. And I'm telling you that if you look carefully enough, you'll *always* find that missing loved one—a new expression of that person's traits, actions, or inactions—in others or in yourself. *The universe conserves.* Knowing this can be comforting in times of sorrow and can inspire you to lift yourself out of the mire of grief.

Using The Demartini Method to Deal with Distance, Divorce, Death, and Other Forms of Disappointment

Reminding yourself that all things are conserved (meaning that they always remain but can appear to you in new forms) can also be a way of balancing your perspective in everyday situations where you may be perceiving loss. I have an amusing game that I play with myself when I'm on the road, when I'm frequently physically "separated" from the woman I love.

When I find myself thinking of her and feeling any degree of "missingness" at the physical distance between us, I just look around. Who has aspects of her character, even her physical appearance or mannerisms? If I pay attention, I can see someone with her spark; another who has her elegant, athletic body; a person with her outgoing, friendly nature; someone else with her beautiful eyes . . . and so on. No, I may not see her replicated in only one individual, but I can observe her in the many people around me, and I feel closer to her, as if she's right there with me. And in truth, she is, just in other component forms.

When I investigated the emotions associated with "loss," particularly in individuals who felt that they'd lost "loved" ones due to divorce or so-called abandonment or death, I discovered something quite intriguing. The feelings of loss, remorse, bereavement, grief, and sorrow only arose in those who were actually unconsciously infatuated with or addicted to some component parts of the person in question—the one they felt that they'd "lost."

They were experiencing what I now identify as a form of withdrawal symptoms from their addiction to those particularly admired aspects. They were actually blindly infatuated with (addicted to) these traits. I found that no one felt these emotions for the disliked, despised, or resented parts of that same person. In fact, they had an underlying sense of relief—almost joy—for the removal of what they hated.

We feel pleasure when we're "freed" from those qualities we resent or when we're joined with the subjects of our infatuation. We perceive sorrow or loss when we come close to something we resent or when we're separated from those parts we idolize. I often call these infatuations addictions and fantasies and the resentments "subdictions" and nightmares.

Now you may ask, "What do we do about these partial perceptions and the feelings that go with them?" Just as before, where I gave you the specific steps for Sides A and B of The Demartini Method, now I'm including precise instructions for completing Side C, which will help you in any situation where you feel as if you've lost someone, whether you're missing a friend or dealing with something apparently more serious, such as divorce or death of a loved one.

If you find yourself making excuses for not completing the process, feeling like giving up, or thinking that it won't work for you, reread the beginning of the chapter on completing The Demartini Method or refer to the Appendix and review the Objections Frequently Posed about The Demartini Method for some inspiration to carry on and get the job done. You can do it!

Side C

Note: A copy of the form used for this exercise is included in this book's Appendix. Here are guidelines for using it:

This part of The Demartini Method is designed to balance your misperceptions of loss or gain by helping you identify the traits you perceive as existing in only one person, acknowledge their existence elsewhere in other forms, see how each version of the quality is both a drawback and benefit to you and others, and realize the shortcomings of the manifestation you've been infatuated with—plus recognize what benefits exist in having the trait exhibited in other ways.

Column 15

— *Purpose:* To precisely define what character trait you feel you gain(ed) from within someone else or yourself by meeting or by being associated with another person.

— *Supporting principles:* You can never gain or lose a characteristic within or around yourself. All human traits are conserved and change only in form.

— *Instructions:* Start in Column 15, "Trait I imagine this person provides or provided to me." Using just a few words (no more than four for each trait), list the qualities that you feel you gain(ed) by meeting or being associated with this person. Write only one trait in each space provided in this column.

For example, if you're using The Demartini Method to help you balance your perspective on a relationship that you perceive as having just begun—someone appears to have entered your life in some way—then record what you now feel that you've gained as a result of becoming acquainted with this individual. You might write something such as: *emotionally supportive, hot sex,* or *life partner.*

The primary question to ask yourself as you complete Column 15 is: **What human trait do I imagine this person provides or provided to me?** This characteristic, action, or inaction could be from any of the seven areas of life. In other words, consider what you think you gain(ed) from him or her in spiritual, mental, vocational, financial, familial, social, and physical terms.

— *Confirm that you're done:* Ask yourself, *Are there any more human traits, actions, or inactions that I imagine I gain(ed) from this person?*

Column 16

— *Purposes:* To identify the form in which the trait listed in Column 15 was occurring *prior to* this person's physical presence in your life; to awaken your awareness of the fact that nothing's ever gained, only transformed, and that all human qualities and life events are present in one or many forms or people and are conserved through time.

— *Supporting principles:* You can never gain or lose a human trait within or around you. All qualities are conserved and only expressed between one or many forms and people. Nothing is ever gained or acquired; it simply exists in a form that you currently don't recognize or acknowledge.

All people receive a balance of characteristics outward from others or inward from themselves to maintain equilibrium. This realization is one of the greatest human discoveries.

— *Instructions:* Go to Column 16, "Initials of people who displayed this trait prior to my association with this person and to an equal degree." In the space to the right of each trait you listed, write as many initials as needed until you're certain that the trait wasn't missing prior to meeting this person.

The primary question to ask yourself as you complete this column is: **Who (whether one or many) displayed this trait to me prior to my meeting or association with this person—and did so to an equal degree?** It's not a question of *whether* this attribute has always been present in your life, but only a matter of *where, who, when,* and *in what form.*

Here's another way to look at this inquiry: **If I felt that I gained someone or something, who or what was the old form?** (Consider whether it's one or many, self or other, male or female, or local or nonlocal.)

Continue until you can honestly see that this property was present to the same degree before you met the person in question, whether it was in similar or different forms.

— *Confirm that you're done:* Ask yourself, *Can I see that this human trait has always been present in a similar or another, different form to exactly the same degree as I perceive that it exists now?*

Or, for someone or some trait that's newly present in your life, ask: *Can I see that this human trait has always been present in a similar or another, different form to exactly the same degree as I perceive that it exists now that I'm with this person?*

Column 17

— *Purposes:* To identify the many drawbacks to the new form of the trait as it's expressed by the person in question; to further dissolve any infatuation, excitement, and elation concerning the assumed gain of the characteristic associated with this individual; to neutralize any infatuation with the quality in general—to avoid minimizing yourself in relation to it.

— *Supporting principles:* Every human trait has two sides, one a benefit and the other a drawback; nothing is one-sided. Every attribute is neutral until someone judges it either helpful or an obstacle, according to his or her own individual hierarchy of values.

— *Instructions:* Move on to Column 17, "How this trait in him or her is/was a drawback or disservice to me." Abbreviate the word(s) representing how the trait, action, or inaction in Column 15 hinders or hindered you (or disserves or disserved you) in all seven areas of life, as well as in the past, present, and potential future.

The primary question to ask yourself as you complete Column 17 is: **What are the drawbacks to me of this human character trait as it's expressed by this person?**

— *Confirm that you're done:* Ask yourself, *Can I see that this trait in him or her has been both a service and a disservice, a blessing and a curse, a benefit and a drawback?*

Column 18

— *Purpose:* To identify the many benefits of the other, previously existing forms of the human character trait so as to release any remaining feelings of gain.

— *Supporting principles:* Every human trait has two sides, one a benefit and the other a drawback; nothing is one-sided. All properties are neutral until someone judges them either positive or negative, according to his or her own individual hierarchy of values.

— *Instructions:* Go to Column 18, "How this trait, as it was expressed in another, previous form, benefited me." Abbreviate the word(s) representing how this prior expression of the attribute listed in Column 15 assists or assisted you.

The primary question to ask yourself as you complete Column 18 is: **What were this trait's advantages to me, as it was expressed previously?** Another way to ask this is: **When this quality was present in another way, what were that form's benefits to me?**

— *Confirm that you're done:* Ask yourself: *Can I see that this trait had equal benefit to me when it was previously expressed in another way, by another person, or in another form?*

Column 19

— *Purpose:* To precisely define what character trait you feel that you've lost (from within someone else or yourself) by meeting or by being associated with this person.

— *Supporting principle:* You can never gain or lose something within or around you. All qualities are conserved and change only in form.

— *Instructions:* Go to Column 19, "Trait I imagine I have lost or now miss." Write the attribute(s) that you think someone else took from your life or that you feel you lost by dissociating or departing from another. The primary question to ask yourself as you complete Column 19 is: **What old character trait do I imagine that I've lost or now miss?**

— *Confirm that you're done:* Ask yourself, *Are there any more traits, actions, or inactions that I imagine I've lost and now miss as the result of this person's departure?*

Column 20

— *Purposes:* To identify the new form in which the property listed in column 19 is now occurring after the old departure and dissociation; to awaken your awareness of the fact that nothing is ever lost, only transformed. All character traits and events are modified and conserved.

— *Supporting principles:* You can never gain or lose a characteristic within or around you; all are conserved and only change expression between one or many forms and people. No quality is ever lost or missing; it simply exists in a form that's currently unrecognized or unacknowledged.

All human beings receive a balance of traits outward from others or inward from themselves to maintain equilibrium. This realization is one of the greatest human discoveries.

— *Instructions:* Go to Column 20, "Initials of people who display this trait after him or her and do so to an equal degree." Write the initials of whomever (one or many) exhibits this feature, action, or inaction now that the person in question isn't here to do so. Keep writing initials until you're certain that the trait is conserved and equally present, although in a new similar or different form.

The primary question to ask yourself as you complete Column 20 is: **Who (one or many) now displays this human character trait, action, or inaction now that the person in question isn't here to do so?** You may also ask: **If I feel that I lost someone or something, who or what took on the new form (one or many, self or other, male or female, local or nonlocal)?**

— Confirm that you're done: Ask yourself, *Can I see that there are new expressions of this trait in my life?*

Column 21

— Purposes: To identify the many benefits to the new form of the trait now being expressed; to dissolve any resentment, depression, pain, remorse, bereavement, and brokenheartedness concerning the assumed loss of the old manifestation; to neutralize any infatuation with the quality in general (remember, when we idolize others, we minimize ourselves); to further dissolve any "crush," excitement, and elation concerning the once-assumed presence of the old quality associated with the person in question.

— Supporting principles: Every trait has two sides, one a benefit and the other a drawback; nothing is one-sided. All is neutral until some human judges something either "good" or "bad," according to his or her own individual hierarchy of values.

— Instructions: Go to Column 21, "Benefits to me of the new form of this trait." Identify and list the first letter(s) of the benefit(s) of the current form of the characteristic. Record the blessings to you—the upside—of this new expression of the old property.

The primary question to ask yourself as you complete Column 21 is: **What are the benefits to me of the newly displayed form of this human character trait?**

Keep listing the first letter(s) of the benefit(s) until you can no longer feel infatuated with the old trait, and you're not grieving a perceived loss of the previously expressed quality.

— *Confirm that you're done:* Ask yourself, *Can I clearly see the benefits to me of the old trait's new form?*

Column 22

— *Purposes:* To identify the many drawbacks to the old form of the trait that was expressed before; to dissolve any infatuation, elation, and/or excitement concerning the previous attribute in order to release any remaining feelings of loss.

— *Supporting principles:* Everything has two sides, one a benefit and the other a drawback; nothing is one-sided. All is neutral until some human judges something either "good" or "bad," according to his or her own hierarchy of values.

— *Instructions:* Go to Column 22, "Drawbacks to me of the old form of this trait." Identify and list the first letter(s) of the many personal downsides of the once-displayed form of this property.

The primary question to ask yourself as you complete Column 22 is: **What were the drawbacks to me of the previously displayed form of this human character trait?**

Keep listing the first letters of the shortcomings until you can no longer feel infatuated with the person's previous expression of the trait in Column 19, and you're no longer perceiving a loss.

— *Confirm that you're done:* Ask yourself, *Can I clearly see the drawbacks to me of the old form of the trait—the one that I was once infatuated with and then thought I was missing?*

Actions to Create More Fulfilling Relationships

— Use The Demartini Method to help you move past whatever feelings you have about someone who has "left" you. Who would be a good candidate? Did you have limited or no access to a biological parent when you were a child? Have you ever gone through a "bad breakup"? Have you divorced or experienced the death of a loved one? If you're still imagining that you missed out on something because of these or any other so-called losses, take the time now to neutralize whatever fantasies you still nurture about others and experience love without regrets. Set yourself free of any relationship baggage.

Words of Power

In love, there is no loss.

Death is an illusion; life just changes form.

There is nothing to fix, but much to cherish.

*I can see all that I care for if I just open my
eyes to the world around me.*

I embrace the new forms of love in my life.

*I balance my perceptions and transcend my
addictions and subdictions.*

※※※ ※※※

CHAPTER TEN

The Three Great Laws of Relating

And the law can only bring us freedom.
— Johann Wolfgang von Goethe

If you break a social law, what happens? In our culture, if you get caught, you're usually warned, reprimanded, or punished. What happens if you break the laws of relating? Do you get punished?

Not really, because you can't break these statutes. You can, of course, live in ignorance of them, which can leave you feeling uncomfortable and unfulfilled. You can flout them and pretend they're not governing your relationships, which may bring you some deluded sense of personal power. *But you can't break these laws—they just are.* They don't change with the times, alter with the rise and fall of civilizations, or follow fashion trends. They're immutable.

This may sound confining, as if we're talking about fate or something or as if we have no choice. And yes, there's some level of constraint. But, as Goethe noted, there's also freedom. When you gain wisdom about how people relate to one another—whether they're romantic partners, parents and children, bosses and employees, friends, or extended family—you experience an incredible new sense of liberty. You *do* have a choice: You can decide to be blinded by your infatuations and resentments, or you can choose to return to the heart of love, where you see the hidden order (which I call divine magnificence) in its entirety.

When I decided to write this book, I wanted to give you a few of what I call the *universal principles of life* and show you how they specifically apply to relationships. My intention is that as you practice what you've learned here, you'll feel more equipped to create the kind of life you'd love, and you'll understand how to do so in collaboration with someone else. Perhaps you've come to view the tangle of feelings, issues, and communication—which are a part of any human partnership—as a divinely inspired web. In time, and with your own attention and intention, you'll be brought more and more into the heart of love, and those around you will be drawn there, too.

In this last chapter, I've summarized the three great laws of relating for you. Use this as a review of all you've learned, to help cement the principles in your own consciousness. Later, it may come in handy as a quick reference whenever you're getting ready to use The Demartini Method or just want a refresher course, perhaps because you're looking to revitalize an old relationship, start a new one, or conclude one with grace.

The Law of Conservation

If you remember your chemistry from high school, you're already familiar with this law, which states that energy can't be created or destroyed but can change its form. In other words, it's a constant and doesn't come and go. Energy is—period.

When you take this out of the laboratory and into your life, you realize that all life is—period. Existence is made up of energy and matter, and while material forms may appear to come and go, the energy remains, transformed and enlivening some new form of matter. Further, human character traits, a type of current, are conserved through time. They may change appearances and show up in new people or situations, but they always exist. They don't come and go, but they do transform.

Perceptions that something's missing—in yourself or someone else—or that one person brings or takes away anything, are merely illusions. When you know that this law governs all energy, you're set free from your limiting viewpoint to see myriad forms of all things.

Nothing's missing, and nothing's gained or lost. Everything remains. Energy is; love is.

The Law of Polarity

If we move on to physics class, we can look at something called wave-particle duality, which is basically just a scientific name for the law of polarity.

You see, light behaves in an interesting way, depending on the kind of experiment you do. Sometimes it displays particle-like behavior, and sometimes it acts like a wave. So is it one or the other? It's both. Physicists refer to "the wave nature of particles" and "the particle nature of waves" when they attempt to describe the nested duality of the nature of light.

The law of polarity states that everything (not just light) can be separated into two wholly opposite parts, and that each of those still contains the potentiality of the other. Particles have the potentiality of waves, up exists with down, white has black, slow is also fast . . . and the same holds true for elation and depression, infatuation and resentment, kindness and cruelty, generosity and stinginess, and so on.

No event is solely beautiful or tragic, just as no person is just good or bad. Labeling things this way may help you talk about them, but it doesn't bring you to the heart of love. Instead, realize that every time you allow yourself into an extreme, you create the equal experience of the opposite. When you acknowledge that one-sidedness is merely a function of perception, not truth, it opens the doorway to seeing the rest of what is. And when you allow yourself to perceive the whole of anything, you're open to the divine perfection of the universe.

Nothing is one-sided; everything contains its opposite. All is love.

The Law of Equilibrium

Sir Isaac Newton revealed that any action has an equal and opposite reaction; forces come in pairs, he said. You can observe a similar phenomenon in chemical reactions. And in life, you've probably noticed that what goes around comes around. Things have an inherent balance.

Although something may appear one-sided in the moment, in time you'll see that there is, indeed, an equal and opposite reaction in that same moment. If someone is criticizing you and attempting to tear you down, for example, you can count on the fact that you'll soon be able to recognize that somewhere, simultaneously, someone else is complimenting you and attempting to build you up.

If you look in the moment, and even over vast spans of time, you see great order. The universe maintains equilibrium and synchronicity.

These three great laws form the backbone of everything in this book. When you consider the myths that have been built up around relationships, it's easy to see that they're all attempts to either ignore or subvert these principles. Your "pursuit of happiness" and belief that everything in your life should be pleasant, fast, and easy is nothing more than the misguided pursuit of one-sidedness. Believing that you need someone else to complete you disregards the great law of conservation, presuming that what you love comes in only one form—and that this is outside yourself.

When you keep these laws in mind, cultural trends can make more sense, too. For example, the American public is currently polarized on many issues, from the so-called war on terror, to the use of natural resources, to personal sexual behavior; and the more radical one side becomes, the further the other side goes in the opposite direction. Until society at large, and the individual in particular, can integrate the two extremes and come to the center point, the culture will remain unaware of the heart of love. Yet when you're humble in the presence of divinity, in recognition of the magnificent order of life, you can have confidence in humanity.

The Demartini Method was designed to assist you in balancing any excesses in your personal life. Its goal is to help you not only in times of crisis, but also whenever you're ready to make a leap to the next level of understanding and love. As I wrote in the first chapter of this book, being willing to do this doesn't "enlighten" you once and for all. Fresh illusions will appear, and you'll be challenged again and again by new things to learn about yourself and how you relate to others.

But you *will* gain wisdom if you choose to use relationships for their true purpose: to help awaken you to the inherent balance existing within and around you. You'll see these three principles unfolding an amazing life before you. You'll be able to acknowledge your own wholeness and magnificence.

I encourage you: Don't just learn these laws; live with them. Let them inspire you toward balance when misperceived circumstances seem to pull you to extremes, when you feel yourself falling into a fantasy or building up resentment, when you're tempted to put another person on a pedestal or throw someone into the pit. Allow yourself to awaken to the divine order of the universe, and you'll find love at the center.

Thank you for inviting me into your life for this brief time. It's both humbling and uplifting for me to be able to share these principles with you and perhaps bring you closer to the heart of love. May I meet you there someday.

᙭᙭᙭ ᙭᙭᙭

APPENDIX

While Filling Out the Form . . .

Think categorically into the seven areas of life: spiritual, mental, vocational, financial, familial, social, and physical. **Think chronologically** into the past, present, and future. When the positives outweigh the negatives, you become emotionally attracted and infatuated (addicted). When the positives don't equal the negatives, you lie. Lies are imbalances. When the positives equal the negatives, you become balanced, grateful, and unconditionally loving. The truth is balance!

(Property of the *Concourse of Wisdom School of Philosophy and Healing*)

Please note that you will benefit from listing at least 20 traits in the first column of each side of the form, and then completing the remaining columns accordingly.

The Demartini Method, Side A

Person:

Date:

Column 1	Column 2	Column 3	Column 4	Column 5	Column 6	Column 7
Trait I most like or admire about him or her	Initials of people who see this trait in me	How this trait in him or her is a drawback or disservice to me	How this trait in me is a drawback or disservice to others	Initials of those who see in him or her the opposite trait to Column 1	Initials of people who simultaneously did/do the opposite trait to Column 1	Benefits that I experience when this person acts out the opposite trait to Column 1

While Filling Out the Form . . .

Think categorically into the seven areas of life: spiritual, mental, vocational, financial, familial, social, and physical. **Think chronologically** into the past, present, and future. When the positives outweigh the negatives, you become emotionally attracted and infatuated (addicted). When the positives don't equal the negatives, you lie. Lies are imbalances. When the positives equal the negatives, you become balanced, grateful, and unconditionally loving. The truth is balance!

(Property of the *Concourse of Wisdom School of Philosophy and Healing*)

Please note that you will benefit from listing at least 20 traits in the first column of each side of the form, and then completing the remaining columns accordingly.

The Demartini Method, Side B

Person:

Date:

Column 8	Column 9	Column 10	Column 11	Column 12	Column 13	Column 14
Trait I dislike or despise most about him or her	Initials of people who see this trait in me	How this trait in him or her is a benefit or service to me	How this trait in me is a benefit or service to others	Initials of people who see in him or her the opposite trait to Column 8	Initials of people who simultaneously did/do the opposite trait to Column 8	Drawbacks to me of this person acting out the opposite trait to Column 8

While Filling Out the Form . . .

Think categorically into the seven areas of life: spiritual, mental, vocational, financial, familial, social, and physical. **Think chronologically** into the past, present, and future. When the positives outweigh the negatives, you become emotionally attracted and infatuated (addicted). When the positives don't equal the negatives, you lie. Lies are imbalances. When the positives equal the negatives, you become balanced, grateful, and unconditionally loving. The truth is balance!

(Property of the *Concourse of Wisdom School of Philosophy and Healing)*

Please note that you will benefit from listing at least 20 traits in the first column of each side of the form, and then completing the remaining columns accordingly.

The Demartini Method, Side C

Person:

Date:

Column 15	Column 16	Column 17	Column 18	Column 19	Column 20	Column 21	Column 22
Trait I imagine this person provides or provided to me	Initials of people who displayed this trait prior to my association with this person and to an equal degree	How this trait in him or her is/was a drawback or disservice to me	How this trait, as it was expressed in another, previous form, benefited me	Trait I imagine I have lost or now miss	Initials of people who display this trait after him or her and do so to an equal degree	Benefits to me of the new form of this trait	Drawbacks to me of the old form of this trait

Objections Frequently Posed about The Demartini Method

While completing The Demartini Method, there may be moments when you feel mentally and emotionally challenged. You may long to give up, throw in the towel, or just plain quit; attempting to answer each question sufficiently and completely in all of the columns will probably try your mental faculties at times. These are normal feelings that will wax and wane as you proceed.

There may even be a few moments when you feel that you just can't go another step, let alone complete the method. The difficulty is more often an internal conflict than an actual inability to think out the answers, though. The key is to not let any of these transient emotions stop you from going through with this important and life-changing process. Keep asking yourself how this exercise will help transform your life, which will give you your own incentive to continue. When your "why" is big enough, your "how" will take care of itself.

You may even find yourself, when challenged, coming up with so-called valid reasons as to why you can't continue or come up with the answers. Most all of these excuses are simply that: excuses. Don't let any of them keep you from completing the method. I assure you that the work and effort will be worth it, once you're finished.

In this section, I've listed some common objections that I've heard from thousands of people while helping them through The Demartini Method. Don't let the disempowered you interfere with your stronger self. Refuse to give up and just keep working. If necessary, go on to another column and then come back later to the one that previously stumped you. No matter what, keep digging into your memory and keep working. Let nothing stop you.

Where there's a will, there's a way. Having the incentive or motivation to continue is the key, and the results will be worth whatever challenge you may think that you're facing. So, just keep going until the method is completed. Your heart will thank you, and so will the people you love.

Excuse: I don't know if I can I do this by myself without anyone's help.

Response: Yes. Thousands of people have succeeded in completing this method beautifully without any outside help. There's certainly no harm in receiving aid, but if the instructions are followed completely, the method takes care of itself while you're working alone.

Excuse: I don't know (or I can't think of) any more answers for a particular column.

Response: Yes, you do know and can think of more, so keep digging into your memories for the answers! It's not uncommon for people to run into momentary mental (memory) blocks while they actively work on this. Don't be alarmed or discouraged; simply continue to concentrate on the question at hand and know with certainty that you have the answer within your mind. (This has been proven by tens of thousands of cases.) Keep going and looking within; giving up isn't an option.

Excuse: I haven't known this person long enough to be able to complete the process.

Response: If you've known the subject long enough to be upset or infatuated with him or her, then you know enough to identify the opposites. Keep working.

When we interact with a person and create our perceptions, we filter out much of what we take in from our conscious mind. We selectively allow in and delete out perceptions that support or challenge our personal values. When we feel that it supports our values, the positive information is allowed into our conscious memories and the negative is stored in our unconscious. In turn, when we feel that it challenges our values, negative data is allowed to surface, and the positive is kept hidden.

All the information is there, yet our values selectively filter what we consciously remember. Sometimes it takes diligent probing to dig out the other, emotionally charged half of the information from our unconscious memories. So it's not that you can't remember, because you can. It's just that you must probe beneath your selective filter. If you interacted with and experienced the person at all, then both positively and negatively charged information is available. All events are neutral and balanced until our conscious values filter gets ahold of them. Keep looking; giving up isn't an option.

Excuse: There's no way you can say that I have the same trait to the same degree as this person.

Response: After examining 4,600 human character traits in one of the largest dictionaries available, I discovered that everyone displays (in some form or another) every known positive and negative quality. Each person's hierarchy of values determines how these attributes appear, but you'll find that they're all there if you inspect closely. We require them to survive in the world, so it's not a matter of *if* you have them; it's a matter of *in what form* you display them. Whatever you see in others you have within yourself.

Keep digging. People often don't want to admit to themselves that they display certain shadowy character traits. Yet no matter how hard you try to rid yourself of certain characteristics, they don't disappear. They simply become repressed or hidden from your conscious memories for a while until they're forced into your awareness.

Our pride often blocks us from seeing our true natures, but it's possible, so keep looking.

Excuse: I don't think I can find drawbacks to some character trait that I believe is good or benefits in something that I believe is bad.

Response: Each quality is actually neutral (neither good nor bad) until some person with a set of projected values labels it; good and bad are merely perceptions. It's up to you to see beyond your own filter and projections in order to get to the truth of the characteristic and discover this inherent balance. In other words, one person's food is another's poison.

By remaining fixated in your initial moral or ethical view, you allow the trait in question to run your life; but by neutralizing your perception, you set yourself free. Keep looking for the drawbacks. Giving up isn't an option.

Excuse: I don't have a problem with anyone.

Response: If you don't have such a challenge, you'd be wise to get on your knees and pray for one. Without something to work on, we die or give up on life. If you're on this earth and have a body, I'm certain you can find someone or something you feel strongly about, so look again.

Excuse: I can't think of anyone I hate.

Response: Maybe *hate* isn't the word to use. Think of someone whom you strongly dislike or who you feel aggravates or frustrates you.

Excuse: I don't want to think of the person that way.

Response: Is that because you want to hold on to your current perception of that individual? The truth sets you free, while your illusions imprison you. Ecstatic fantasies are accompanied by torturing nightmares. When you realize that you're complete in and of yourself, you'll have no reason to fear writing down those traits, for each one will be balanced by its opposite and appreciated and loved.

Excuse: My therapist said it was better for me to hate this person.

Response: I'm not necessarily telling you to disobey your therapist. But he or she may not be familiar with The Demartini Method and, therefore, may not know how it can help you dissolve your anger and get on with your life. Carrying around such feelings has been shown to disturb your health and other areas of your life. If, after you finish, you'd prefer to go back to being upset, you certainly may.

Excuse: I've already worked out all my problems with the person.

Response: If you still describe them as past *problems,* then there's likely to still be some charge associated with them. Would you like to have them not run your life anymore? Then let's keep working.

Excuse: I haven't done as much as that person has.

Response: What you see in others is a reflection of you. Who has seen you do that? Who else? Don't let yourself lie to yourself. Look again—sometimes you've done the same thing in a different form.

Excuse: I've never done that.

Response: If you discover that you're stuck on a particular event that you believe you haven't done in the physical sense (such as *I've never killed anyone*), look into all seven areas of your life and find the ways you've "killed" others with your thoughts, words, or actions. Remind yourself that there are many ways to "kill" someone and that everyone has every trait in some form.

Excuse: You don't understand that this person really hurt me.

Response: I understand that you currently feel that this person hurt you. Now, would you like to have that emotion continue to run your life, or would you love to be set free? If you complete this process, you'll no longer perceive him or her as having injured you. Instead, you'll realize that this individual also provided you with an equal opportunity for pleasure. If you'll just continue working the process, you'll set yourself free and discover how this damage can be dissolved and you can become re-empowered. Every minute you spend thinking about your pain reduces a minute that you can feel set free. Realize, too, that your perceptions caused you to suffer more than their actions did.

Excuse: There's no way I'll be able to "balance" them.

Response: That's what many people say when they begin. But so far everyone has been able to do so completely in the end. I'm certain that you will, too—so keep working. Instead of thinking about how you can't, just get working on balancing them.

Excuse: This person is evil. There's no way I'll be able to find any good in him or her.

Response: Everyone has two sides, and all events have both benefits and drawbacks. What you see in others is simply a reflection of yourself. If you don't want this person to continue to run your life, then keep working.

Excuse: I already forgave this person for the terrible things he or she did to me.

Response: If you still imagine someone as having done something terrible to you, then you still have an emotional charge toward him or her and are letting yourself be controlled by another. You can still liberate yourself further, for the truth of love sets you free. Anything you fear or condemn will continue to run your life until you embrace it. So keep looking for the benefits until you have nothing to forgive and only feel love and appreciation.

Excuse: But I don't want to love and appreciate this person.

Response: It has been my experience that the very people we feel this way about are the ones who are reminding us of the parts of ourselves that we haven't yet learned how to appreciate. Those you say that you don't want to care for are actually the ones that you *do* want to be able to cherish from within. This is because others are our reflections. Deep inside our hearts, love is patiently waiting to surface. You have nothing to lose by feeling affection for them. When you can do so, you can also embrace the part of you that they represent.

Excuse: I'm not close friends with this person anymore.

Response: That's fine. If you choose not to be close to this person, that's your decision. From taking tens of thousands of people through this amazing method, it's been my experience that they're able to love and appreciate others so much more than if they carried the burden of having to avoid or reject them. The process gives you the freedom to have people in or out of your life with greater equanimity. They deserve to be loved for who they are, just as you do, and this method enables you do exactly that.

Excuse: I think I picked the wrong person to fill out The Demartini Method on, so I doubt I'll get anything out of it.

Response: You can do The Demartini Method on anyone and still benefit, but it's wisest to complete it for someone who still pushes your buttons the most.

Excuse: I'd like to start on someone else.

Response: Don't begin again until you've finished the process for this individual. It's wiser to complete one than to half complete two. Don't move on unless you truly feel that you perceive the other person as only a button pusher.

Excuse: I didn't get enough sleep last night, so I'm tired and sleepy.

Response: Stop writing for a moment, stand up, and go for a brief walk to get your entire body moving. Have a light snack and some water if you're also hungry. Then sit back down and close your eyes. Think about what you're truly grateful for in life (which will help open your heart, clear your mind, and revitalize you) and meditate for 15 minutes, remaining in a sitting position while taking deep, full breaths. When you're done, then get back to completing the method.

Excuse: I'm worn out and can't go on.

Response: This will pass. Just keep working, unless, of course, you had no sleep last night. If so, why don't you meditate for 15 minutes? This will help you feel refreshed. Then get back to work—I promise that it will be worth it.

Excuse: I'm hungry.

Response: If you're truly hungry, go get a small protein snack, and then come back, get to work, and complete the method. But be sure that this isn't an avoidance mechanism on your part. If it is, just get to work.

Excuse: I don't feel well.

Response: If you feel woozy and need to vomit, feel free to do so . . . and then come back and get to work. Many people have felt dizzy or slightly ill until they finished, and then they were fine. Just keep going.

Excuse: I have a headache.

Response: Ask someone close to you to massage your scalp, have a chiropractic adjustment, take a natural aspirin, or meditate for 15 minutes and then get back to completing the method. Generally, headaches will subside and pass if you just keep working toward your goal.

Excuse: I can't think—or don't want to think—of anything else.

Response: Yes, you can. I hear this excuse weekly, but everyone completes the method. The results are worth the effort. The ideas will come in spurts, so keep working. You can do it! (By the way, the brain doesn't stop thinking.) I know you can complete this. Make sure that you look at all seven areas of life.

Excuse: I'm mentally shut down and my brain is fried.

Response: Stop for just a moment, go for a brief walk, move and stretch your head and neck, write down ten ways in which completing this method will help transform your life and enable you to fulfill your highest values, and then get back to completing the method. You'll tend to shut down whenever you can't see how this will help you meet your most important goals. In order to say that you're brain-dead, your brain actually has to be alive. Keep working—I assure you that this is worth completing.

Excuse: I'm not sure that the effects I've experienced will last.

Response: Whatever character trait you've truly balanced through this process will no longer be the button or emotionally charged quality that runs your life. If you leave the method incomplete, that same characteristic will keep troubling you until it's truly brought to balance and completely collapsed. You aren't designed to stop growing mentally and emotionally, so expecting yourself to have no more strong reactions is unrealistic. But a goal to no longer be set off by any one specific trait is reasonable. Complete the method and watch the results.

❇❇❇ ❇❇❇

ABOUT THE AUTHOR

Dr. John F. Demartini is an international speaker and consultant who breathes life and enthusiasm into his audiences with his enlightening perspectives, humorous observations of human nature, and practical action steps. When he speaks, hearts open, minds become inspired, and people are motivated into action. His gentle, fun, and informative teachings mingle entertaining stories with transformational wisdom and insights. His trailblazing philosophy and revolutionary understanding are reshaping modern psychology and business and transforming the lives of millions. As a retired chiropractor, researcher, writer, and philosopher, his studies have made him a leading expert on healing, human potential, and philosophy.

Dr. Demartini is the founder of the Demartini Human Research and Education Foundation, which includes the Studies of Wisdom research and the Concourse of Wisdom educational divisions. He is also the creator of The Breakthrough Experience® seminar and originator of The Demartini Method® and The Great Discovery™. He has written several dozen books, including the three bestsellers *Count Your Blessings: The Healing Power of Gratitude and Love; The Breakthrough Experience: A Revolutionary New Approach to Personal Transformation;* and *How to Make One Hell of a Profit and Still Get to Heaven.*

Articles and feature stories about Dr. Demartini and his insightful personal and professional development methodologies have appeared in numerous international magazines and newspapers. He's appeared on hundreds of radio and television news and talk shows and in several film documentaries. As a presenter, Dr. Demartini has shared his transformative principles and methodologies in conferences with business executives, health professionals, financial managers, and consultants working in the field of human consciousness, and he has presented alongside many of the most well-respected speaking professionals today. As a pioneer on the frontier of human consciousness and an explorer of the ultimate nature of reality, he's a leader in the field of psycho-spiritual development and transformation.

Dr. Demartini also is a private consultant, advising people from all walks of life on personal and professional development and achievement. These include Wall Street financiers, corporate executives, health professionals, politicians, Hollywood stars, and sports personalities. His many clients use his expertise and wisdom to assist them in keeping their lives, health, relationships, attitudes, and business acumen steadily on track.

For more information:
(888) DEMARTINI or (713) 850-1234
Fax: 713-850-9239
www.DrDemartini.com

❋❋❋ ❋❋❋

Hay House Titles of Related Interest

I Can Do It® Cards: Affirmations for Romance,
by Louise L. Hay

Love Notes: 101 Lessons from the Heart (includes music CD),
by Jim Brickman, with Cindy Pearlman

*Love . . . What's Personality Got to Do with It?: Working at
Love to Make Love Work,* by Carol Ritberger, Ph.D.

*A Relationship for a Lifetime: Everything You Need to Know
to Create a Love That Lasts,* by Kelly E. Johnson, M.D.

Rising in Love: Opening Your Heart to All Your Relationships,
by Alan Cohen

*Secrets of Attraction: The Universal Laws of Love, Sex, and
Romance,* by Sandra Anne Taylor

All of the above are available at your local bookstore,
or may be ordered by contacting Hay House
(see last page for info).

We hope you enjoyed this Hay House book.
If you'd like to receive a free catalog featuring additional
Hay House books and products, or if you'd like information about
the Hay Foundation, please contact:

Hay House, Inc.
P.O. Box 5100
Carlsbad, CA 92018-5100

(760) 431-7695 or **(800) 654-5126**
(760) 431-6948 (fax) or **(800) 650-5115 (fax)**
www.hayhouse.com® • **www.hayfoundation.org**

Published and distributed in Australia by: Hay House Australia Pty.
Ltd., 18/36 Ralph St., Alexandria NSW 2015 • *Phone:* 612-9669-4299
• *Fax:* 612-9669-4144 • www.hayhouse.com.au

Published and distributed in the United Kingdom by: Hay House UK,
Ltd., 292B Kensal Rd., London W10 5BE • *Phone:* 44-20-8962-1230
• *Fax:* 44-20-8962-1239 • www.hayhouse.co.uk

Published and distributed in the Republic of South Africa by:
Hay House SA (Pty), Ltd., P.O. Box 990, Witkoppen 2068
• *Phone/Fax:* 27-11-706-6612 • orders@psdprom.co.za

Published in India by: Hay House Publications (India) Pvt. Ltd.,
Muskaan Complex, Plot No. 3, B-2, Vasant Kunj, New Delhi 110 070
• *Phone:* 91-11-4176-1620 • *Fax:* 91-11-4176-1630
• www.hayhouseindia.co.in

Distributed in Canada by: Raincoast, 9050 Shaughnessy St.,
Vancouver, B.C. V6P 6E5 • *Phone:* (604) 323-7100 • *Fax:* (604) 323-2600
• www.raincoast.com

Tune in to **HayHouseRadio.com**® for the best in inspirational talk radio
featuring top Hay House authors! And, sign up via the Hay House USA
Website to receive the Hay House online newsletter and stay informed
about what's going on with your favorite authors. You'll receive
bimonthly announcements about Discounts and Offers, Special
Events, Product Highlights, Free Excerpts, Giveaways, and more!
www.hayhouse.com®